# FEEDBACK REVOLUTION

### FROM WATER COOLER CONVERSATIONS
### TO ANNUAL REVIEWS

## HOW TO GIVE AND RECEIVE EFFECTIVE FEEDBACK

### POSITIVE! CANDID! TIMELY! REVOLUTIONARY!

PETER MCLAUGHLIN

JAVA CREEK PUBLISHING

*FEEDBACK REVOLUTION*

*ISBN: 978-0615890883*

*Giving feedback is not for amateurs.*
*Is there any more difficult task than giving effective feedback?*
*If there is, I can't imagine what it would be.*
*If you think giving feedback is easy or "straightforward," then you are*
*hyper-shitty at giving feedback.*
*No one is open to poorly proffered feedback. No one = No one.*
*Giving feedback is a skill to be studied, practiced and mastered as much/*
*as carefully as, say, playing the piano.*
*Begin with a planet-class training course [on giving feedback],*
*require EVERYONE to take it, provide mandatory annual refresher.*

Tom Peters' Tweetstream, August 2013

*To get candor, you reward it,*
*praise it,*
*and talk about it.*
*Most of all, you yourself demonstrate it in an exuberant and even*
*exaggerated way - even when you are not the boss.*

Jack Welch, *Winning*

*If you are going to criticize someone you should always walk a mile*
*in their shoes first...*
*Because when you do give them feedback, you will be a mile away*
*and you'll have their shoes...*
*That's pretty damn good advice.*

Peter McLaughlin

# TABLE OF CONTENTS

# HOW TO READ THIS BOOK

My first piece of advice —

Don't read this book until you've taken the FEEDBACK SELF-ASSESSMENT SURVEY.

In fact, don't read any more of this section until you've taken the survey. Go ahead: I'll be waiting for you at the end of the survey.

# FEEDBACK SELF-ASSESSMENT SURVEY

Take the assessment and review your answers on the spectrum of giving feedback.

Think of a specific setting — work, home, community — and rate each statement.

Rating: 1=Never, 2=Rarely, 3=Sometimes, 4=Often, 5=Always

1. I understand the importance of giving both positive and negative feedback.      1 2 3 4 5

2. I think I would give feedback more often if I knew how.      1 2 3 4 5

3. I offer feedback on performance in a timely manner.      1 2 3 4 5

4. As I think through my feedback, I make any changes or adjustments based on how the feedback will be delivered — face-to-face, phone, email, etc.      1 2 3 4 5

5. When I share my observations as part of giving feedback, they are so clear that anyone hearing them would readily come to the same conclusion.      1 2 3 4 5

6. I am able to show appreciation for the other person even when I am disappointed with the behavior or performance.      1 2 3 4 5

7. I thank the other person when I have finished providing feedback.      1 2 3 4 5

8. I easily accept that other people may have a different perception from mine.      1 2 3 4 5

9. I offer feedback only when I have adequate physical energy and a positive attitude. 1 2 3 4 5

10. I tend to be very specific in the feedback I provide. 1 2 3 4 5

11. I ask for permission before I give feedback. 1 2 3 4 5

12. We both leave the meeting with clear expectations. 1 2 3 4 5

13. I know and plan for my best time of day for giving feedback. 1 2 3 4 5

14. My primary goal for providing feedback is to help the other person improve. 1 2 3 4 5

15. I am not judgmental when I give feedback. 1 2 3 4 5

16. I use a respectful tone when I give feedback. 1 2 3 4 5

17. My feedback is more dialogue than monologue. 1 2 3 4 5

18. I check my attitude before I offer feedback. 1 2 3 4 5

19. When I give feedback, I think about "what's in it for them." 1 2 3 4 5

20. I think about what is the best time and location for the person receiving the feedback. 1 2 3 4 5

21. When preparing feedback, I keep in mind generational differences among my direct reports. 1 2 3 4 5

22. I prepare the content of my feedback with specifics before I give it. 1 2 3 4 5

23. I try to leave a "positive emotional wake" whenever I give feedback. 1 2 3 4 5

24. I am good at checking my emotions before spontaneous feedback sessions.                1 2 3 4 5

25. I believe I could get better at giving feedback if I practiced.                1 2 3 4 5

---

**YOUR SCORE** _____

---

115—125 Fabulous: This survey verified what you already do — you should be teaching a course. Give yourself a raise and a pat on the back.

105—114 You're good! But not great. Change a few things and watch yourself skyrocket — pick three things to change.

90—104 We still love you, but here's some feedback: If you put your mind to it, you can achieve greatness — just do it!

25—89 You need quite a bit of work, but it can be fun: Take the items that are easiest for you to improve on and work on them first. Good luck.

Now that you've taken the survey...
What's the best way to read *Feedback Revolution?*
The quick answer — and we hope an accurate one — is that this book was created to be read with:
- Enjoyment
- An open mind
- An eagerness to learn
- An awareness that the approach to feedback contained in this book is not only revolutionary but is designed to be adapted and evolved by *you*

- An understanding that while the byline on the book is mine, the contents now belong to you — make them your own!

But it was also created to be read in the way that best suits you.

## THE PATH THAT BEST SUITS YOUR NEEDS

The book is organized in a linear fashion and makes steady A-B-C progress, but we're all aware that business, or life, doesn't always proceed so smoothly. Perhaps you need immediate insights, advice, and strategies for a specific area of feedback, or a specific type of feedback challenge.

Because the book covers so much territory, I've put together a detailed Table Of Contents that can steer you, at a glance, to the concepts and sections that best suit the problem at hand. *Feedback Revolution* rests upon a broad range of experience, research, and observation, and the book reflects that. Chapters and sections, though as self-contained and self-explanatory as possible, build upon and reinforce one another. While there are plenty of individual "trees" here, there's also a rich and well-developed "forest." It is my hope that you will find value in seeing both.

Above all, I have worked to make every page light, accessible, and entertaining, as well as informative. We all face such an unceasing — and increasing — torrent of information that our goal was to make every bit of the information I present as open and easy to absorb as possible. Let me know how I did — I not only write about feedback, I also love receiving it.

## TIPS, TOOLS, & TACTICS

Each chapter — and, where appropriate, specific sections of an individual chapter — closes with a series of "feedback basics": focused and targeted suggestions, proven approaches to feedback problems, "try this" ideas, and more.

Many of these are derived from my work with Marjorie Mauldin, founder and CEO of Executive Forum, on the creation of our **iLoveFeedback** program; all have been tested in real-world business environments, including my own business clients.

These lists take the following form:

- **TIPS:** Proven nuggets of advice on the relevant feedback topic
- **TOOLS:** Practical and easily introduced or adapted hands-on materials to enhance your feedback environment
- **TACTICS:** Brief suggestions and strategies for putting the Tips and Tools into practice

# INTERLUDES

In the middle of each chapter you will find a brief Interlude. The relevance of these sections to the surrounding chapter will be obvious, but the Interludes serve another purpose as well.

*Feedback Revolution* draws upon cutting-edge and breakthrough brain research, showing how it relates to and enhances both giving and receiving feedback (as shown in *Brain Rules* by John F. Medina, Ph.D).

It turns out that brain research provided some feedback into structuring this book as well.

There is a gathering body of research showing that humans absorb information best in 10-15 minute increments, with a break between learning sessions.

It struck me that this lesson could be applied to the organization of the book, and, after some reflection, I came up with the idea of Interludes.

The word Interlude itself comes from the middle Latin *inter* plus *ludus* — which means to enter play. The Interlude served as a kind of intermission so that you could process what you were seeing, much as in medieval banquets. During such banquets, an interlude between each course would present the diners with a piece of music, perhaps a portion of a play, or a jester, or an acrobat — something to allow guests the opportunity to digest their food while also diverting and entertaining them before the next course was served.

The Interludes here are intended to provide the same function — a chance for you to take a brief break with a diversion before returning to the full course.

*Bon appétit!*

## CARTOONS AND HUMOR

I begin each chapter with a cartoon, and humor plays a large part throughout the book. Our intent is to set the tone for each chapter with a smile — and a reminder that a good cartoon can sum up its subject at a glance. I feel sure you'll take more than one glance at the cartoons we've included.

## LOGS

Throughout the book I've included extracts from my Feedback Logs, as well as several from Margie Mauldin. These are brief narrative explorations of a particular event or episode that we've experienced. They are intended as sorts of "mini-Interludes," brief breaks from the larger narrative, intended to entertain, inform, and cast a personal light on the material being explored.

## BACK TO THE BEGINNING

As I asked a couple of pages ago:
*What's the best way to read this book?*
You know the answer —
*The way that suits you best.*
Good reading — and Good Feedback!

*Feedback is always present-centered
but future-focused.*

# INTRODUCTION

# THE REVOLUTION IS
# BEING TELEVISED

What do President Abraham Lincoln, supermodel Tyra Banks, and former GE CEO Jack Welch have in common?

At first glance — not much.

One of the three is a woman, so obviously gender is out.

Two of the three are wealthy, but Lincoln's poor financial circumstances rule out money as the common factor.

Only one of the three had a beard — so facial hair isn't it.

What, then, do they share?

All three understood the critical importance of effective, candid, specific, constant feedback, far more than a component of an annual performance review or a response to a situation — and all three arrived at that understanding early in their careers.

In fact, a case can be made that their understanding of the value of real feedback — and the ways the real thing differs dramatically from what passes for feedback in many companies — was what made them so successful in their careers.

Even Abraham Lincoln's beard, as we'll see in the course of this book, had as much to do with feedback as it did with not shaving.

So why aren't more people putting effective feedback to work?

Probably because they don't know what effective feedback is.

If you don't know what something is, how can you be expected to talk about it?

The way in which feedback is practiced in most organizations gives a clear indication of why most business feedback is less than effective:

- Annual performance reviews that follow a strict and often inflexible formula and, in the most extreme cases, a script
- Lack of training in both giving and receiving feedback effectively
- An almost ritualized dread of feedback sessions
- A dangerous misperception of feedback as consisting primarily of criticism, and of criticism as primarily negative in nature
- A tendency to consider a paycheck the only positive feedback employees need
- An unwillingness on the part of executives, managers, and supervisors to *invite upstream* feedback — and to make the invitation open and constant

Sound familiar?

It should — these and similar observations and insights are all but universal among the companies and organizations with whom I've consulted on feedback and related issues.

Of course, in order to get to those observations and insights, the executives, managers, and supervisors I worked with had to first understand what effective feedback is, and why it's so vitally important.

*Feedback* — timely, specific, two-way feedback — is among the most effective communications tools we possess. And while we all possess the ability to master the arts of giving and receiving effective feedback, most of us lack the skills necessary to do so.

And we lack the skills because most of us don't actually know what the elements of effective feedback are.

This book was created to correct that situation, and to correct it in an enjoyable, inviting, and above all, practical way.

This book was created to give you the tools you will need to create a Feedback Revolution in your company.

But people like Abraham Lincoln, Tyra Banks, and Jack Welch — and others who understand what feedback actually is, and how to use it — are also in exceptionally short supply. Which is why effective feedback itself is in exceptionally short supply — and why it is more needed, and *more valuable*, than ever.

This book was created to change this situation.

This book's purpose is to clear away the fog and misunderstandings that surround feedback as typically practiced and replace them with clarity, tools, and techniques for putting *real* feedback in place in your business.

In short: This book's purpose is to help you create a FEEDBACK REVOLUTION, just like the title says.

Feedback Revolution will:
- Show you what effective feedback is — and what it isn't
- Identify the key elements of effectively presented feedback
- Help you establish a "feedback culture" at your company
- Teach you how to receive feedback as well as give it
- Provide strategies for integrating new levels of feedback into your existing performance review structure
- Establish criteria for effective, memorable, profitable feedback sessions
- Present scientific evidence showing how feedback works best — and how to identify those habits that may be hobbling your own feedback
- Help you move from dreading feedback sessions to a posture of welcoming them — I Love Feedback rather than I Hate Feedback

*Why should you learn to love feedback?*

Because properly prepared, presented, and received feedback is among the most valuable sources of information, insight, understanding, and knowledge in any career or industry, in classrooms at every level of education.

Feedback Revolution rests upon experience, observation, and research — every tool or technique presented here has been tested in business and has demonstrated consistent effectiveness in the real world.

Some — perhaps much — of what I say about feedback will be new to you.

It was new to me too, once.

I started thinking about feedback a long time ago.

That was a good thing, as I discovered when I received a request from a client: Could I develop a "Feedback Program" for their company?

I was sure that I could develop such a program, and that it would be an effective one — I just wasn't sure whether I *should*.

I discussed the matter with my son Peter McLaughlin, Jr., who headed up research and program development for the McLaughlin Company.

Feedback seemed pedestrian and boring. I felt that putting together such a program might be like writing an instruction manual for assembling cheap furniture. (This was far from the last time I would discover how wrong I was in the ways I thought about feedback.)

But there was something else.

> Thank you for your entertaining presentation on The Power of Feedback. I was fortunate enough to be able to attend, and found myself recommending your tips and recommendations to friends and colleagues. I believe the feedback message invaluable, and trust that those of us who attended the session are practicing the lessons learned to foster a company that embraces the **iLoveFeedback** program.
>
> Elaine T. Cloutier,
> Lean Six Sigma Coordinator,
> Visteon

I knew that I wasn't particularly good at feedback. I can see now that I was, in fact, a bit of a "feedback coward." I did not like giving people bad news (even if they really needed it). I was reticent to give people good news (even if they really deserved it). I was the one who would not tell people what I really thought, but instead would show them the door with "the company has decided to go in a different direction" speech.

Despite my initial hesitations, we decided to take up the challenge. After much research and work with the HR and Training Departments at Visteon, the largest auto parts maker in the world, my Fortune 200 client, we built and delivered a Feedback Program for the company's 2,400 managers and supervisors. Our program included the necessary follow-up to help feedback endure as part of the company's new performance management culture.

The results were overwhelming.

This was partly because the need for such a program was much greater than Visteon had anticipated, and partly because the managers now had some tools to work with and the motivation to do so.

I'm not sure we achieved our overarching goal, but I think we came close. That goal was to change their mindset about feedback, and change it in the way I described above, to help them go from:

- I Hate Feedback
  to
- **I Love Feedback**

In other words: learning to truly appreciate giving and receiving effective feedback with grace (as Ernest Hemingway might say) no matter how challenging the circumstances the feedback addresses.

*That* is the revolution — the *Feedback Revolution*!

It's a revolution that took place within myself, and my own mindset, as well as within my client's culture.

I found myself becoming better at giving and receiving feedback, and as I did so my fascination with the subject deepened and broadened.

I made notes and explored additional avenues of research, refining my thinking, and the speeches and presentations based upon it.

As I began writing this book, I was invited by Margie Mauldin, president of Executive Forum, a 26-year-old Denver company that brings a broad range of executives together several times a year for intense and enjoyable sessions exploring a variety of topics, to do a presentation on feedback.

At the end of what was a very well-received and provocative session, Margie approached me and suggested that my approach to feedback could form the basis of an effective and important training program.

Working together, Margie and I developed the **iLoveFeedback** training program.

**iLoveFeedback** has proved to be especially valuable in providing its participants with hands-on, practical training in the elements of effective feedback and how to deploy them in business.

*Feedback Revolution* places the **iLoveFeedback** training program and its elements in a larger historical and cultural context, with added exploration of the ways in which cutting-edge brain research confirms and extends the effectiveness of the **iLoveFeedback** approach.

You'll find Margie's own voice in her personal Logs in the book; her insights are striking and memorable.

And that's how *Feedback Revolution* and the **iLoveFeedback** training program came to be.

But wait!

As the TV hucksters would say: There's MORE!

## TUNING IN TO FEEDBACK

At the beginning of this book project, as I was writing the first few pages, I took a time-out to refresh my brain with some exercise; and while on the treadmill, I turned on the TV and there was Tyra Banks.

And guess what? She was giving feedback to a potential winner in *America's Next Top Model*, her popular TV program.

Watching her deliver specific, clear feedback was an epiphany to me. The more I watched, the more I saw her, and her colleagues, giving well-thought-out feedback to both winners and losers.

It occurred to me that any manager of a company watching this show could derive great coaching lessons from her content and style. I'm sure many thousands have watched that show and never said to themselves or anyone around them, "What a great example of how to deliver feedback."

Examples of great feedback are right in front of us, and we don't see them...and that is another part of the revolution.

*The revolution is being televised...*we just have to see it with fresh eyes. And it is crucial that we do come to see it.

Visteon's understanding that feedback was a necessary and vital part of a well-run company set it apart from most businesses, a fact that still holds true.

Feedback — or the lack of it — is for many, and maybe most, companies the elephant in the room that nobody talks about, the naked emperor everyone is afraid to confront about his lack of clothing.

Businesses know they need better feedback; they're just not sure of how to go about developing and implementing it.

We are surrounded by examples of feedback everywhere (TV and sports especially), but we need a catalyst to help us be aware of it and bring it into our lives and organizations. That is what this book is all about.

That's what the *Feedback Revolution* is all about.

And it's about time companies joined the revolution.

Fortunately, whether the companies know it or not, much of the groundwork for a feedback revolution already exists.

Marshall McLuhan once famously stated, "When any revolution occurs, it has already happened." In our minds and thoughts, consciously or unconsciously, we've been preoccupied with the problems leading up to the action. When the action happens, the revolution is over.

I can safely "predict" a Feedback Revolution in business because it has already happened and is being televised in the form of sports programming and reality TV.

The reason we don't "get it" in business is because there is no road sign pointing to the television, identifying relevant programs, and saying, "Hey! You should be doing *this* in your companies (and families, for that matter)."

To be fair, those relevant programs don't have signs proclaiming themselves FEEDBACK SHOW either. Yet reality shows, and sports' vastly increased openness about the nature of coaching — further extended by color commentary that's often quite detailed in terms of coaching — give us hours of effective feedback, right there on our TV screens every week. Some of it is lousy, some good, some great, but we can learn from it all if we pay attention.

And we had better start paying very close attention.

Turn on, as McLuhan said, and tune in (but don't drop out).

# INTERLUDE

## TYRA BANKS AND STEVE JOBS:
## FEEDBACK LESSONS GOOD AND NOT SO GOOD

O ften during a consulting engagement I will recommend that people watch Tyra Banks' popular TV show, *America's Next Top Model.*

*Tyra Banks*

I always enjoy and appreciate the looks of puzzlement and curiosity I get in reply — but not as much as I enjoy the looks of insight and understanding I receive when I explain why.

If you haven't seen *America's Next Top Model*, its premise is simple: Every week a group of ambitious young models is judged by Tyra Banks — and every week one of the models fails to measure up and is cut from the roster.

Those who don't measure up know they are losing their prospects of being on the cover of *Glamour*, as well as thousands, if not millions of dollars.

And they're given as much help as possible by the show's star — Tyra's feedback is constant...up to the moment the contestant strides down the walkway on her own.

In giving feedback, Tyra is empathetic yet specific about the contestants' strengths and weaknesses; she gives them ideas and actions to work on in hopes of improving their future chances. Tyra Banks has been giving feedback like this for the 10 years her show has been in existence.

Can you imagine how good you could be as a manager if you practiced feedback that much — and had millions of people watching as you gave your feedback?

Tyra's success is borne out by her net worth, which hovers at about $90 million, and the fact that her TV show has lasted this long.

Steve Jobs never had a reality TV show — and if he had, feedback would not have been one of the lessons he taught.

Tyra Banks' $90 million is but a drop in the late Steve Jobs' Apple barrel. Tyra Banks is no Steve Jobs, but in some important ways, Steve Jobs was no Tyra Banks. Luckily for him, Apple wasn't built on his ability to give feedback that was based on empathy and graciousness. *Steve Jobs'*

*Lessons in Effective Feedback* is a book that will never be written. Steve Jobs was more attuned to inventions, ideas, and vision than people.

In his truly great biography, *Steve Jobs*, Walter Isaacson writes that James Vincent, the producer of the first iPad ads, was attacked by Jobs — who told him, "Your commercials suck. The iPad is revolutionizing the world, and we need something big. You've given me small shit."

"Jobs went ballistic," Vincent recalled.

*Steve Jobs*

Ann Bowers, Steve Jobs' Director of HR in the '80s, was in charge of "reprimanding Jobs after his tantrums, and tending to the wounds of his coworkers. He was very impetuous and difficult, but the journey was the reward."

Tyra Banks teaches lessons in feedback that are easily transferable and adaptable to virtually any business situation. Steve Jobs' management and feedback styles were transferable to no one.

None of us will ever be Steve Jobs — he was one-of-a-kind, and our world is the better for him and the innovations he introduced. And I suppose that being the Michael Faraday of the last century and the Walt Disney of the first decade of the current one earns Steve Jobs a bit of a pass when it comes to his feedback style. He was the founder and CEO and chief visionary, but you can be thankful he wasn't your manager.

On the other hand, most of us will never walk a runway as a model, either — but all of us can learn lessons in empathy, specificity, and absolute candor from a supermodel who puts those lessons on display on TV every week.

# FEEDBACK TV

The incredible irony of feedback being all around us is that we don't see it because we don't call it feedback.

We call it REALITY TV, even though the very essence of the many and varied reality TV shows is simple: performance and feedback.

Take a look at the best reality TV shows — Tyra Banks' (as mentioned) America's Next Top Model, the Food Network's Chopped, even American Idol or Dancing With the Stars. Beyond its admittedly effective "You're fired!" shtick, The Apprentice presents very effective, systematic feedback to its contestants.

Watch even a few of these programs and you'll see that beneath the showbiz glitz and glitter, beyond the criticism of poor performances, there is almost always a strong strain of encouragement, explanation, understanding, teaching. Even contestants who don't "make the grade" are told how they can improve their performances and, most importantly, how they can develop and build upon the strong skills they already possess.

Best of all — and in my opinion a sterling example of great feedback in practice — is Tyra Banks' show. While she could certainly have built a show around her physical appearance and success, encouraging contestants to "do what she did" in order to "be like her" — a template essentially employed by Donald Trump every week — Tyra took a different approach.

She honestly and precisely evaluates each contestant's strengths and weaknesses — and then shows them how to develop their strengths, not to try to imitate hers. It's not her job — or, I suspect, her interest — to turn a would-be Tyra Banks into a *better* would-be Tyra Banks.

Instead she does something far harder, far more rewarding — and far more entertaining.

She works with the contestants, helping them discover themselves, test themselves, believe in themselves.

And she does it without either sugarcoating her feedback or couching it in the sharp-tongued (and often devastating) put-downs that Trump and many other reality show stars use to show how great they are.

It's a marvelous example of real feedback and *effective* feedback — which is always *worthwhile* feedback.

Nobody learns anything worthwhile from a put-down performer, or a screaming coach, or a relentlessly belittling manager or constantly hyper-critical parent, spouse, or partner.

Actually, that's not quite true.

What we learn from the negative approach to feedback includes:

- What a self-important jerk a coach or manager or TV star can be
- How rotten our jobs are
- How unlikely it is we will ever do anything right in their eyes

And, worst cases, but hardly uncommon:

- How futile it is for us even to try
- How easy it is for us just to give up

How did Tyra Banks come to break the mold of what a reality show host offers contestants? From feedback — and, in her case, from *negative* feedback.

In her case, as she told *60 Minutes* during a break from her Harvard-based executive training studies — that's right, modeling, starring on TV, running a business, *and* attending Harvard! — she has always been underestimated by those around her.

Told "You can't do this" or "You won't succeed at that" or "This isn't for you" or "Nobody's ever done that before; why do you think you can?" Tyra digs in, draws upon her carefully cultivated and developed strengths and resources, and proceeds to prove the naysayers wrong.

And it's that determination, that awareness of her abilities and how she can use them to best effect that she seeks to instill in participants on her show in terms of *their* skills, talents, and abilities.

They learn from *her* who *they* are. Will they become "America's Next Top Model?" Maybe — but probably not.

Will they emerge from Tyra's feedback as stronger individuals with a better-honed sense of themselves and their potential? *Definitely!*

*That's* feedback.

And our television listings, virtually every night of the week, contain example after example of feedback factories masquerading as entertainment programming. Most of them are nowhere near as good as Tyra's show, but take a look at any of them, and you'll be surprised at what you can learn about feedback in the course of an hour.

# (RE)INVENTING FEEDBACK

The examples cited above, from the unlikely avenues of reality TV and sports, put me in mind of how inventions, like mindsets, arise from putting unlike things or ideas together...the coin punch and the wine press gives us the printing press; a bell plus a clock gives us an alarm clock; a copier plus a phone gives us a fax; a cell phone plus an operating system and a display screen gives us smartphones.

Understanding that what's really going on with reality TV and sports coaching is feedback gives us a whole new mindset for approaching feedback. From fear and loathing to curiosity and confidence...to loving to give and get feedback.

We can see that if we change our mindset about feedback in business, we can learn to see it not as something to "get it over" (until next year's review season) because we dislike it...but to embrace because we understand the incredible benefits not only for those we work with but for ourselves in every aspect of our lives.

If we learn to love feedback...giving it and receiving it...we grow in confidence levels and optimism.

We become true leaders.

# WHY READ THIS BOOK

Some of feedback's unlikely catalysts are found in each chapter of this book.

Chapter One reveals sports as the ultimate feedback factory, and shows how coaches went from yelling to teaching (although they still yell, but now with much better content and instruction; modern coaches even listen occasionally). In many ways, sports is where the Feedback Revolution began.

Chapter Two shows why feedback is the "elephant in the room" that most businesses acknowledge only rarely (annual performance reviews, generally), and shows how you can transform it from an invisible elephant into a very visible and very prized part of your company culture.

But it's not the only place. Chapter Three shows one of the great lessons from new research in positive psychology, proof that no matter what criticism is to be rendered, putting on your positive oxygen mask is the best way to get ready. I use data from some very good research to focus you on delivering a minimum of three or more positive affects — statements, gestures, asides — to every negative affect for great feedback results.

Until now, no book on feedback has used brain science as a major contributor to understanding and communicating with others. In Chapter Four I take you through some important brain science findings to show that if you have a way to understand how you process information, and by extension how others process information, you'll become much better at asking good questions and starting dialogue. In this chapter I also show you a specific program, Emergenetics, developed by Geil Browning, Ph.D, and Wendell Williams, Ph.D, that gives you tools for better understanding individuals' thinking and behavior styles.

In Chapter Five, research data about the multi-generational workforce are used to give you a one-up in confidence for providing and receiving feedback with and from people older or younger than you. This will span the range from the very loyal *"why isn't it like it used to be?"* folks to the *"whatever"* types. Delivering and receiving feedback across generations is a total chance for your growth as well as theirs.

Chapters Six and Seven explore the effects of the technological revolution — everything from email to Twitter — on feedback, and also remind us of the virtues and benefits of traditional media — paper, telephone — as well as good old face-to-face conversations. To be effective, feedback must be adapted to the technology you'll be using for its delivery. You don't want to approach a Webinar with your team the same way you approach a one-on-one conversation with a single member. Yet that Webinar can be just as inviting and, in fact, almost as personal as a face-to-face conversation. In these two chapters I show you how to make sure that your feedback retains a human face, whatever the technological interface you're sharing with your recipients.

The title of Chapter Eight says it all: *How'm I Doing? The Art of Receiving Feedback.* Legendary New York Mayor Ed Koch is still best known for his favorite question — the question that gives this chapter its title. The question is just as important to you — and your business. It is just as vital that you learn how to accept, and especially how to *invite*, feedback as it is for you to give it.

Chapter Nine examines the role of creativity in feedback including strategies and tactics for enhancing your own creativity and raising the creativity level of the feedback you offer. Are you surprised by the subject? You won't be after you read this chapter. After a brief reminder that *yes, we all really are creative*, I take a look at the role creativity plays in enhancing and enriching feedback, and offer some insights on how you can raise the creativity level of your feedback by raising and exploring your own creativity.

Chapter Ten looks at the nature of a true "Feedback Culture" and gives practical tools to help you prepare to meet with direct reports (or your kids, for that matter), taking into account everything from time of day to blood sugar levels (especially your own) and "Feng-Shui-ing" the physical environment. "Preparing a face to meet the faces you will meet," as T. S. Eliot would say. Getting ready is everything, and sometimes you have only five seconds...use the time wisely.

I end with a coda that explains why feedback is really "feed-forward." Just don't turn there yet.

Let's start at the beginning.

As a way of putting on your own oxygen mask first, I hope you followed my suggestion and began by taking the Feedback Self-Assessment in the previous pages before you read anything else in the book. (You may already have taken it, as recommended in HOW TO READ THIS BOOK — if, so, bravo! If not, go take it now.)

The self-assessment questionnaire will open your mind to the possibilities of where the Feedback Revolution can take you and, at the same time, focus your attention in a very different way on your own journey. Be brutally candid in your answers. This questionnaire is geared toward helping you FACE THE TRUTH.

*FACING THE TRUTH* is what effective feedback, and this book, is all about. Face the truth in your answers to the Feedback Self-Assessment, and you'll have begun to learn what feedback really is, and how it can change your world.

I'm confident, of course, that you'll learn even more about feedback from the pages of this book. So take the questionnaire and then join me in Chapter One, where we're going to look at exactly what feedback is, what it isn't, and how to tell the difference.

Welcome to...

# THE FEEDBACK REVOLUTION!

*Peter McLaughlin*

The definition of Feedback that I used while developing the concepts in the book:

Feedback is information that is shared with another person for the distinct purpose of improving results or relationships. Effective feedback is not venting, shaming, or giving in to excuses.

*I never yelled at my players
much. That would have been
artificial stimulation,
which doesn't last very long.
I think it's like love and passion.
Passion won't last as long as love.
When you are dependent on passion,
you need more and more of it
to make it work.
It's the same with yelling.*

John Wooden,
legendary UCLA basketball coach

*I hope you like sports metaphors.*

## CHAPTER ONE

## SPORTS – THE ORIGINAL FEEDBACK FACTORIES

I've already lived and worked through one *Feedback Revolution*. Of course, I didn't know that it was a revolution at the time.

But it was. I can see that now that I was inadvertently at the heart of it, and the lessons I learned there made me eager to spread the revolution.

What revolution? This one:

> *Feedback is good for you!*
> *Feedback is good for your team!*
> *Feedback is good for your company!*
> *Feedback is good for business!*
> *Feedback is good for your family!*
> *Feedback is something you can learn to love!*

In fact, I *do* love feedback, and I am convinced that by transforming the ways in which feedback is currently practiced (or not), and replacing them with cutting-edge tools that are built upon the latest research and insights about the brain that I'll present in this book, any organization can make itself more productive, more effective, more successful, and more fun.

If it's true, as Jack Welch has noted, that the absence of effective feedback is among the largest of problems, then why is feedback so poorly practiced in our businesses and institutions?

The easy answer is that they don't know any better.

But the right answer is that most of us haven't seen good examples of effective feedback techniques.

Fewer still have lived and worked in a true *culture of feedback*, or even been aware of such cultures and the enormous benefits they generate.

However, as you saw in the Introduction, those examples are all around us.

Where can we find those good examples being habitually put into practice?

Watched any sports events lately?

You should.

Successful sports teams, at whatever level, and in whatever sport, are *feedback factories*.

## FEEDBACK LOG: PETER

I was hired by the Washington Capitols of the National Hockey League to consult with the coach and help build a solution to get the team into the playoffs. I had co-authored a book, *Mentally Tough* (with Dr. James Loehr, renowned sports psychologist), and though I had never been a hockey player, my charge was to help the team understand what mental toughness was all about and see if we could change some habits.

We reviewed the situation with the coach, and it was easy to see the problem: The team was ahead in many of the contests going into the third period, then lost. They couldn't put the opponents away...they choked in the final period.

The feedback was candid and straightforward, and included two solutions that had not been anticipated but that were immediately apparent. Both had to do with energy:

The players were physically tired...so their trainer set a new plan to upgrade their exercise schedule.

Secondly, they were emotionally negative. Any setback was greeted with fear (anxiety that is always accompanied by scattered thinking) and anger (which leads to rigidity in both brain and body).

The prescription came through a series of workshops, with the team giving them a picture of what a "performance zone" looked like and how to attain it in the tough times — how to turn stress into positive action and teamwork. We changed their ideas of what a pre-game meal looked like; we changed their exercise routine; we treated the third period as if the score was 0-0 (no matter how far they were ahead) and it was attack time. Play to win; don't play to "not lose." They seemed to receive it well, but I wasn't sure as there was a bit of "why should I listen to a guy who never played hockey" attitude... totally understandable; I would have felt the same.

They made it into the playoffs, and who knows how much, if any, credit I deserved. I loved the assignment because of the challenge, energy, and fun. Going on the road with a National Hockey League team is its own reward.

*Peter*

# FEEDBACK DOESN'T HAVE TO BE LOUD

That first Feedback Revolution I referred to was the transformation of athletic coaching over the past few decades. And since the most recent of those decades have seen the dramatic and long overdue arrival of women's athletics as the equal of men's, sports analogies and examples speak clearly to both genders. This is a good thing both culturally and because athletics has been a vital proving ground for the transformation of feedback.

> Am I drawing too much of a correlation between sports and feedback? I assure you that I'm aware of the concern — but there's also some pretty impressive research to back up my sports focus.
>
> Steven Forness, EdD, Distinguished Professor Emeritus at UCLA and a leading expert in emotional disorders in children, is well-known not only for the breadth of his research, but also for being the principal of the hospital school for children admitted to the UCLA neuropsychiatric institute, one of the leading psychiatric hospitals in the United States. His school had five classroom programs, from preschool to high school, each staffed by a team of teachers and assistant teachers.
>
> Looking back over 40 years of his research teams at UCLA, Dr. Forness noted that most of his team leaders had been female — and that the very best of them had played team sports at some point during their education.
>
> They each instinctively seemed to understand not only the effectiveness of teamwork, but also the importance of integrating feedback to each member of the team, from assistant teachers to lead teachers.

If you're past a certain age, you may remember coaching as primarily a matter of... *yelling.*

That's what coaches did: they yelled. (Oh, some of them, the best of them, did more than that, but it's the yelling that most of us remember.)

"You're doing that wrong!"

"Don't do that!"

"Are you stupid?"

"Who told you *you* could play this game?"

(And so on, endlessly at least until the coach either gave up or developed laryngitis.)

Up to a point, being yelled at can be a powerful motivator. None of us want to be yelled at; most of us will make an extra effort to avoid being the target of a loud voice. Sports histories are filled with famous athletes chuckling ruefully about the rough treatment they received at the hands — and, more specifically, the *voices* — of their often equally famous coaches and managers.

Yelling got things done. But it wasn't effective feedback. Why not?

Because effective feedback, the kind that improves both performance and self-confidence, is hard to deliver in a loud, angry, exhortatory voice.

Some things *can* be delivered through shouting: Motivation, sure (and again, only up to a point).

Self-*consciousness*, undoubtedly: How would you feel being yelled at in public over a simple mistake? (If it ever happened to you, whether in an athletic context or not, you know you'll never forget it.)

Fear, unquestionably: Those same sports histories are likely to quote more than a few coaches or managers *bragging* about how much their players feared them.

You get the picture.

By the late 1970s, a number of coaches, psychologists, and others were beginning to develop a very different picture of what athletic effective coaching called for.

What it called for was *feedback* — well thought-out, well-intentioned, well-prepared, well-delivered feedback.

## FEEDBACK LOG: MARGIE

Sometimes you have to fiddle a bit before you "tune in to the feedback station." This was a point — and a metaphor — that was brought home delightfully during an *iLoveFeedback* program not long ago.

As we reviewed the "Get Smart" step in *iLoveFeedback*, a lively woman suddenly shouted out: "I get it! I get it!"

What exactly did she get? We all wanted to know, and she was eager to tell us:

"I've been listening to the wrong station!" she exclaimed. "I've been tuned to WIIFM — What's In It For Me!"

Her smile grew even wider as she said: "I need to change to the right station: WIIFT — What's In It For *Them*!"

She was receiving the signal loud and clear — effective feedback is *always* about the person receiving it.

*Margie*

Today, we can see that the success and increasing importance of sports psychologists is a reflection of how much we've come to understand about the relationship of effective feedback to our mental and emotional health, which in turn exerts a dynamic effect on athletic performance.

As I'll show you, our understanding of mental and emotional health also includes the physical health and performance of our brains, as well as our psychology. It's all inextricably interrelated, as good coaches and sports psychologists know — and as more and more executives and managers are beginning to learn.

> Feedback is information that is shared with another person for the distinct purpose of improving results or relationships. Effective feedback is not venting, shaming, or giving in to excuses.
>
> *(From the* iLoveFeedback *training program.)*

## GOOD SPORTS

If you've ever had a really good coach, you already know what I'm talking about.

Good coaches tell you what exactly you're doing wrong and show you how to correct your performance.

Good coaches also tell you what you're doing right and show you how to make those aspects of your performance even better.

Athletes at every level, from preschoolers to Hall of Fame professionals, rely on their coaches to see what the athlete himself or herself cannot: *performance in context.*

Think about what's going on around an athlete in, for example, a football game. The individual athlete has his responsibilities during a particular play, has responsibilities to the team, must track and respond to the rapidly shifting variables that are put into motion with the snap or kick; the crowd is roaring — and it all takes place in a few seconds, with not many seconds before it's time to line up for the next play.

(Remind you of anything? I've had business days that are just as hectic and chaotic — without the cheering fans — and I'm sure you have too.)

The team's coaches, and the cameras, can see the player's performance in the context of the game: shouting — a loud voice is still part of a good coach's arsenal, and always will be — instructions, corrections, and, frankly, the occasional obscenity.

It is in the post-game review sessions, and the practice sessions before the next game, that what the coaches saw is transformed from on-the-fly, win-this-game instructions to carefully and precisely presented feedback.

In practice, it's a beautiful thing to behold.

And I mean literally in *practice.*

# INTERLUDE

## FROM PAUL REVERE TO PEYTON MANNING: IN FEEDBACK, TIMELINESS IS KING

In his book *The Tipping Point*, Malcolm Gladwell cites a story about Paul Revere paying stable boys to give him daily feedback about any changes in the movement of the British troops. Revere figured that if there were going to be any attacks on the American militia, they would start with the British "saddling up."

*Paul Revere*

While sitting in the tavern with his fellow revolutionaries (the tavern was Paul Revere's office, as it has been the office of most of history's great revolutionaries), the word came from the stable that the British were getting ready to ride.

As Gladwell puts it, Paul Revere "was the logical one to go to if you were a stable boy on the afternoon of April 18, 1775 and overheard two British officers talking about how there would be hell to pay on the following day."

Armed with the feedback the stable boys provided, Paul Revere set out for Lexington that night — and the famous **"Midnight Ride of Paul Revere"** entered history and legend.

One might say that the Revolutionary War was won by the American revolutionists because of "timely feedback" versus the inevitably dated feedback of the British. Always having to go across the ocean for permission on any big assaults or decisions eliminated one of the most vital elements of effective feedback — *timeliness*.

Switch to modern-day "Wars of the NFL" and look at the Denver Broncos' Peyton Manning, certainly one of the greatest quarterbacks of all time. And yet, after 14 seasons in the NFL, he feels that he still needs people giving advice and helping him maintain a fresh attitude and new ideas; he, too, pays for feedback. (Technically the Broncos organization pays Adam Gase, his former quarterback coach and now the offensive coordinator, to give him specific and unceasing feedback.) As Peyton said in the Denver Post (9/15/12), "I think the older you get, the more important it is to have a guy to watch your fundamentals, certainly go over defenses and reads and progressions, but also to go over your fundamentals, your throwing mechanics."

But Peyton Manning also knows how to *give* feedback, a skill never more on display than in the October 15, 2012 game against San Diego when he led his team back from a scoreless first half, 0-24, to a 35-24 double-digit victory. It was the first time in NFL history that had been accomplished. Still settling into his role as quarterback for the Broncos, Manning used feedback to guide his teammates' responses and patterns to plays he called, showing them what *he* wanted, how *he* does it, all while giving them plenty of positives for the performances his feedback was reshaping.

*Peyton Manning*

The results speak for themselves — and so now do the NFL records.

Now, think of Peyton Manning as a manager of your company. If the way he studies his teammates is any indication, he would know all the tendencies of his direct reports, their strengths and weaknesses, and he would ask for *their* feedback to help him communicate more effectively with them. From the feedback of the top brass, he would know the direction the enterprise is moving and would, in turn, give feedback to his team so they (like his offensive line) would know their parts as participants in the grand scheme.

If, like Paul Revere, we would seek out feedback and, like Peyton Manning, we would put aside our own egos and anxieties about receiving and giving on-time feedback, our own "Feedback Revolution" would be off to a great start.

# PRACTICE MAKES PRECISION

Every year I would go out and watch Mike Shanahan, now coaching the Washington Redskins, and his staff put the Denver Broncos through pre-season practice sessions. I looked forward to it every time — and every time I learned something new about feedback.

If you've never been to a college or professional athletic team's practice session, you've missed a terrific opportunity to see just what feedback is, how effective feedback is presented, and how quickly feedback's messages can be delivered — and received.

And all of it in an environment that can put a three-ring circus to shame.

A hundred different things are taking place at once. The field is divided into sections for offense, defense, and special teams. One group is working on kicking, another on passing formations. Footballs are hurtling in multiple directions. Assistant coaches call out commands and instructions.

Chaos?

Hardly!

Watch a practice session carefully — keeping your eye on the practice itself, and especially on the coaches — and you'll quickly realize that what you're seeing is an exceptionally well-organized flow of energy — and information.

Every single play, and every single player, receives feedback from the coaches. Not just Shanahan, who can move 120 players to new positions in a matter of seconds with a single command called through his huge boat horn, but, more importantly, from 15 to 20 assistant coaches.

There is an exceptional level of energy in the air — and every bit of it is freighted with feedback.

Feedback continues with video reviews in the team's classroom.

Feedback is constant and continuous.

Feedback is the norm.

*Everything* is about feedback.

Feedback *itself* is the *environment* in which the practice takes place.

An athletic team's practice session is a perfect example of a feedback factory, with every moment devoted to improving performance, correcting errors, seeking the optimum.

Every single executive, manager, and supervisor, whatever his or her business or industry, should spend an afternoon or two watching a sports team being put through its practice paces. If you're like me, you'll feel your managerial skills put to shame by the level of highly specific, highly effective feedback a coach such as Mike Shanahan delivers. He gets more done in two or three hours than most businesses accomplish in a week.

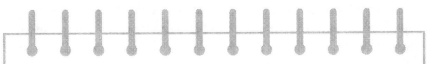

## FEEDBACK LOG: PETER

Some years ago, I was the coach of the Regis University tennis team. One of our players lost three matches in a row in the third set. Everything was going great until crunch time; then the fear and anxiety hormones kicked in. (The results of these anxious moments hit you both mentally and physically. You lose your range of motion and begin to "short-arm" your tennis strokes.)

He asked for feedback, and we talked about how he was feeling doing these points. He reported that his thinking became scattered, so he went defensive hoping for his opponent to make enough mistakes for him to make it through.

It is in the post-game review sessions, and the practice sessions before the next game, that what the coach has seen is translated into effective, targeted feedback for the player(s).

We settled on a new plan: a strategy that would take his mind off "winning or losing." When a match got close, he was to hit every stroke to his opponent's backhand. That was his focus, everything to the backhand...don't worry about winning; his "game within the game" was to see how well he did — you guessed it — hitting to his opponent's backhand.

His play improved almost instantly because he had a plan for any tight moments, and his confidence grew in all aspects of his game. That plan over the next year became a habit, an unconscious response to stress. What is great about developing certain new habits is that they can become what psychologists call "keystone habits." They result in your changing other habits almost automatically...you become a different person.

When my tennis player became "mentally tough" in tennis, changing fear into challenge, he changed his life by becoming more confident in all aspects.

"We are what we repeatedly do." —Aristotle

*Peter*

# FEEDBACK JUST *IS*

One of the things you notice at an athletic practice is the degree to which the players are not only receptive to the feedback they're receiving, they are *dependent* upon it. They know that their success depends on solid, constant, no-holds-barred feedback. They don't get worked up about it — usually, anyway — and certainly not in the ways so many of us in business do. They understand that without feedback, their performance suffers.

*With* feedback, though, they grow and improve as athletes; they find their way to the highest levels of excellence they can achieve.

And they do so because they have come to understand — through feedback and its effects on their performance — that the feedback they're receiving does not fall into positive or negative categories.

To the athlete, feedback simply *is*.

Every bit of it is beneficial, whether the player is receiving specific comments on strengths ("Good read on that last pass!") or areas that need improvement ("Pick up the pace; you're moving too slow!"). They know they need to hear it all.

The best athletes already know they're good — they wouldn't be playing for the Broncos or the Redskins, for instance, if they weren't. So they don't need to hear general praise. Rather, the praise is highly specific, reinforcing particular skills, and the feedback aimed at improving problem areas is even more so.

The players know that if they don't get this kind of feedback, they won't know what areas to improve on. They won't get better. And it's every athlete's ambition to do better.

This is the same as it is, or should be, for every business executive.

One of the lessons of athletic coaching, particularly during the fast-paced action of a game, is that coaches get to the point quickly and immediately. They provide the feedback — the players return to the contest. In-depth, broad-based reviews wait for the post-game debrief or the pre-game strategy session.

It's much the same in business. Formal reviews and in-depth conversations take place once a year, perhaps once a quarter. But the need for feedback remains constant, and the best executives know this.

The ongoing day-to-day "during the game" feedback that managers and supervisors give is dramatically enhanced if it supports — and is both reinforced and extended by — those thorough, deep, and comprehensive strategy sessions known as "performance reviews."

Robert Heller, author of *Andrew Grove: The Innovator Whose Methods Supercharged the Silicon Revolution*, points out that Grove, one of the founders of Intel, understood this well:

*"A manager can also exert high leverage by an activity that takes only a short time but that affects another person's performance over a long time (eg: a properly prepared performance review)."*

The difference is that athletes love feedback or at least respect it — and respect it deeply because they know what it can do for them and their team.

Most business executives actually *fear* feedback (or don't give it the respect or time it deserves) because they know what feedback, as practiced by themselves and their company, *hasn't* done for them or their business.

For instance, if you work at a company that has no feedback culture, or whose culture defines feedback as an almost always negative thing, news that the boss wants to see you is unlikely to generate the same reaction that an identical invitation would engender at a healthy, feedback-friendly company. If the only time anyone hears from the boss is when there's bad news, it's a safe bet that no one ever wants to hear *anything* from the boss.

The distance between the two perceptions is telling — and correctible.

But in order to make the correction — to transform your organization's feedback processes and procedures from something dreaded into something welcomed, expected, and even loved — you'll need to learn what feedback *really* is.

It's a lesson I have been sharing with businesses for years, but it's a lesson that I originally learned — where else? — in athletics.

## BACK TO SCHOOL

Coaching athletic teams at the high school and college levels, and later as a consultant to an NHL team, wasn't exactly part of my plan. But neither are so many of the best things that happen to us.

In fact, I have no doubt you'll discover that as you get better and better at *providing* feedback, you'll also be learning more and more about your company and your employees. In my case, the lessons in feedback began arriving when I was a first-year teacher and coach.

I remember, coaching a freshman football team, when the quarterback pointed out to me that everybody knows that the purpose of freshman play was to toughen up the new guys by way of hardnosed block-and-tackle running plays.

But my quarterback was a terrific passer for a freshman, and he had excellent receivers. He also knew that the opposing teams, having never faced a freshman team using the passing game, would be unprepared for freshman passes — and vulnerable.

It was an excellent suggestion — and an excellent example of how to give feedback to a superior (in this case his coach, me). He not only made his point and offered his suggestion, he included a decidedly appealing potential benefit. Bear that in mind when passing, as it were, feedback up the line.

(His suggestion was not only well-presented, it was right on target. We didn't win every game we played that season, although we did come close.)

## TEAMS WORK

Gradually, over the course of the next few years and coaching jobs, I began to see that by approaching players from a relentless — and relentlessly enthusiastic — position of *teaching* them how to become better athletes, players, and team members, the players got better, and so did their teams.

And more importantly, I saw the players' enthusiasm levels begin to rise sharply.

They were excited.

They were motivated.

They were *having fun.*

And so was I.

Watching a group of young people become a true team — as individual players learned that no matter what they thought of the guy in the next position, they had to work *together* — began to teach me, at least unconsciously, lessons in group dynamics that continue to serve me in business decades later.

My increasing awareness of the difference in energy levels and enthusiasm in a well-coached player as opposed to a fearful one sparked an interest in how our brains respond to feedback.

The teacher in me was delighted as well. The most effective athletes are students of their sport as well as players of it. By helping my players become students of themselves as well as of football or tennis or hockey, I watched these young people develop levels of self-confidence and self-understanding that they carried with them from the playing field or tennis court to other aspects of their lives.

It quickly became clear that this sort of coaching brought enormous benefits beyond putting together effective sequences of plays and winning games.

One of the most rewarding of these was hearing players begin to open up, to become more comfortable with their abilities — and with their deficiencies.

I remember the first time I heard a player, a defensive cornerback, in the midst of a game say, "Coach, I just can't keep up with that guy. You need to put somebody faster on him."

The "traditional" coach's response might be something along the lines of, "Don't you give me CAN'T! There's no room for CAN'T here! Get back OUT THERE and STAY ON HIM!"

After which, the player would return to the field, continue to be unable to keep up with HIS opponent, often with disastrous results — and more yelling.

The *teaching* coach, on the other hand, sees the player's statement as an honest admission of a *team* vulnerability, an opportunity for a corrective adjustment.

It's like that great movie, *Remember the Titans*, where a player insisted to the coach that he be allowed to step aside for another player who was better equipped to deal with the situation on the field. The point is — the player who stepped aside had been well-coached. It was *feedback*, as well as the desire for victory, that led to his decision.

You're not going to get that sort of honesty from players — or direct reports and co-workers or family members, for that matter — who are afraid of you, your shadow, and everything else you represent.

You're going to get that sort of honesty only from team members who know that you have both their interests and those of their team in mind.

Performance, constant improvement of skills, and continual development and refinement of abilities are all vital aspects and central goals of effective feedback — but so is an *absolutely honest and timely assessment and self-assessment of current abilities and their immediate consequences.*

This is vital during a big game — but unless you've carefully prepared the player (or employee) by providing constant, informed, teaching feedback, you're not going to get it.

Because the players *don't get it.*

My players got it.

And it was thanks to them, and the quarterback's willingness to offer feedback to me from the very beginning, that *I* got it.

Not that we won every game — although we did get to the Indiana State quarterfinals for freshman football.

Coaching teams of young football and, later, tennis and hockey players, taught me that there are lessons to be learned from every game, not just the triumphant ones.

There is more to this lesson than the familiar aphorism that "we learn more from failures than we do from success." Probably we do, but in order to get more from the lesson, you have to be willing to dig.

You have to make sure that your team members are willing to dig as well.

And — the neatest trick of all — you have to help your team members learn to love the process.

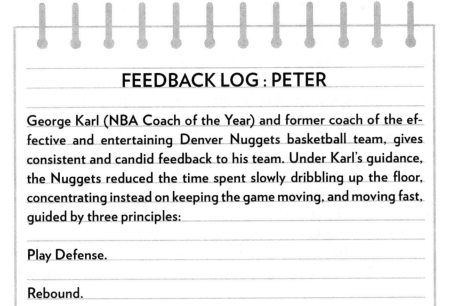

## FEEDBACK LOG : PETER

George Karl (NBA Coach of the Year) and former coach of the effective and entertaining Denver Nuggets basketball team, gives consistent and candid feedback to his team. Under Karl's guidance, the Nuggets reduced the time spent slowly dribbling up the floor, concentrating instead on keeping the game moving, and moving fast, guided by three principles:

Play Defense.

Rebound.

Run.

The Nuggets' "transition" offense took some time and a lot of specific feedback to accomplish. The "no superstar" Nuggets are one of the top teams in the Western conference.

George himself got his great feedback from sports outside of basketball. He learned from the Spanish soccer team who ran and passed to keep opponents off balance; a couple of NFL teams went to uptempo, no-huddle offense following the never-stop University of Oregon's example.

The faster you play, the less time defense has to set up — so a transition offense run by a fast and quick team upsets the balance.

*Peter*

Personal feedback is all around us — until we leave school.

Why is it that after receiving nearly constant feedback in school — tests, grades, comments on papers, report cards — from kindergarten through, for some of us, advanced degrees, even the idea of feedback seems to disappear from our lives, with the possible exception of an often-dreaded annual performance review?

Many of the people I've spoken with in the course of preparing this book and the **iLoveFeedback** training program admitted that they'd never experienced good, consistent feedback at any of the other companies they worked at.

Most of them further owned up to having no idea what effective feedback really is.

There weren't any college courses — or even sections in other courses — on feedback in business.

They had no examples to learn from.

And if they didn't know what it was, they didn't know what it *really* was that they were missing — only that they were missing *something called feedback.*

That sort of vacuum can be disastrous, and often is, as we've all seen with both companies and individuals.

But that sort of vacuum can also be viewed as an opportunity to be filled.

To be filled by a *Feedback Revolution.*

Starting now.

# TIPS, TOOLS, & TACTICS

TIP: Feedback doesn't have to be loud.

TIP: Everything is about feedback.

TIP: Feedback is never about hierarchy or position; it is *always* about helping the recipient, and the overall project or responsibility, do better.

TIP: Feedback is *information*, an opportunity to teach, learn, and grow.

TOOL: Give the feedback questionnaire at the front of this book to your direct reports. What do *they* think effective feedback is? What's *their* assessment of the current state of feedback at your company?

TOOL: Keep a *Feedback Log* of your own. It needn't be as elaborate as the log entries here, but even a series of telegraphic notes about particular feedback sessions can help you track the effectiveness of your feedback.

TOOL: Add a "feedback given" notation to your calendar, planner, or agenda. This can be a simple "FB" with the recipient's initial; even such a brief will let you review at a glance when you gave feedback, just as your log will show in greater detail the type of feedback you gave.

**TACTIC:** Lighten up a feedback session from time-to-time. Feedback *can* be fun — and sometimes it needs to be.

**TACTIC:** While effective feedback is never about hierarchy, don't forget that hierarchies are in place. When offering feedback to a superior, be sure to include carefully enumerated business benefits along with the feedback itself.

**TACTIC:** Find out how many members of your team played sports. Ask them about the coaching styles they experienced, and what they learned, both from their coaches and from the style of feedback those coaches offered.

**TACTIC:** Keep your emotions as calm as possible, especially when presenting negative feedback.

*It requires a very unusual mind
to undertake the analysis of the obvious.*

Alfred North Whitehead

*I'm right there in the room, and no one even acknowledges me.*

## CHAPTER TWO

## FEEDBACK – THE ELEPHANT IN THE ROOM

Even before I began delivering seminars and courses in how to offer effective feedback, and how to create a culture of feedback, it was becoming clear that companies knew, sometimes only vaguely, that many of the issues they faced could be addressed and resolved with improved communications. But what sort of communications?

Most of the companies I worked with had tried various approaches:

- Increased frequency of forms-based reports
- Detailed memos
- Redesigned and reconfigured internal communiqués
- Telephone conferences
- Video presentations
- Recently, software programs and apps have been added to the mix
- And more

You get the picture — over the years you've probably gotten the memos and seen the videos!

Every one of these initiatives is well-intended, and some of them may have even produced results.

But the effort involved in establishing and implementing such initiatives can all too often mask the situation that prompted the *need* for them in the first place.

That situation is, frankly, a lack of feedback — and, more than that, a failure to understand what effective feedback is and how it is used.

*That's* the elephant in the room — not that the companies called it that.

In fact, most companies didn't call their lack of feedback anything at all. As with the elephant in the room, most of the executives knew there was an issue, but it was not something anyone wanted to talk about.

The existing structure and procedures in many, if not most, organizations made it very easy to avoid the subject.

That's because within those structures and procedures are plenty of things that are inaccurately considered to be feedback.

Some of them, as we're about to see, may even be labeled as feedback.

You can label an elephant a whale, and that doesn't change the fact that it's still an elephant, whether or not anyone talks about its presence in the room.

## FEEDBACK LOG: PETER

A few years back, a call from Visteon — one of the largest automotive suppliers in the world, with more than 70,000 employees, located outside Detroit — marked the beginning of this book. Visteon's head of HR had received an employee survey that put "ability to give clear feedback" as one of the top needs for the 2,400 managers, located in the Detroit headquarters. HR said the influx of a new generation of workers, combined with older employees, had created chaos. Feedback (and especially the undetected need for understanding what it was and how to do it) was "the elephant in the room."

Visteon was putting together a performance management system and asked if my company could come up with a new, company-wide approach to "giving and receiving feedback," and make that approach part of Visteon's system.

We created the program and a corresponding training manual and best practices guide. One of the points of clarity that came out of this process was that the *ability to give clear feedback* was an essential part of leadership development.

The unintended consequence of giving timely feedback was the development of self-confidence, something few foresaw, including me. The more the managers worked with their direct reports, the more both participants gained confidence in themselves.

In the beginning, feedback is an act of courage; but with repetition and coaching, most managers quickly develop a deep appreciation for the benefits feedback offers.

The training booklets, surveys, and research I did for this project became the beginnings of *FEEDBACK REVOLUTION*.

*Peter*

## FEEDBACK PERSPECTIVE

Every business issue, large or small, can be approached from a **Feedback Perspective**.

What's a *Feedback Perspective*?

Simple!

It's a perspective that's built upon effective and fully understood feedback on the part of all parties.

That means that you, your direct reports, their direct reports, as well as your superiors are all:

- Engaged in a conversation deliberately aimed at discovering and enhancing the best qualities required for success all around

---

## PAGING DOCTOR FEEDBACK!

Every page in this book is a product of experience and feedback:

1. My experiences and studies of feedback in business, athletics, and education
2. Constant feedback between me and my editor, Keith Ferrell
3. The author and the editor have never met face-to-face
4. The process involved 18 months of phone, email, txt, and Web conferencing

As you can see, *Feedback Revolution* was built by our practicing what the book preaches — we experienced a daily Feedback Revolution of the virtual variety!

In the course of writing this book, for example, we established a relationship that both rested upon the feedback core values the book presents and also put those principles into daily practice.

We quickly became relaxed about offering candid feedback about chapters, pages, even specific words. We created our own small feedback culture, and the book and our relationship are far the better for it.

To use another "money where your mouth is" metaphor, the creation of FEEDBACK REVOLUTION was very much a case of walking the walk as talking the talk.

I wouldn't have it any other way. And neither would my editor.

---

In a true *culture of feedback*, everyone also understands that discussion, commentary, and conversation focused on specific aspects of company operation and employee performance are vital and *rewarding* elements of the *business* — whatever the day-to-day, quarter-to-quarter, year-to-year nature of that business might be.

That's a large step for most organizations — no wonder Jack Welch sees it as a process that takes years.

It's also a large concept to swallow all at once, so let's break it down.

Here's a single, simple question whose answer will give you a glimpse of what feedback can accomplish, and how a feedback culture can begin to be created.

Ask yourself:

- How would my business be changed if every manager met with each of her or his direct reports for an in-depth conversation *four times a year?*

I've tried this any number of times with any number of managers and executives. They agree almost immediately that more frequent in-depths with their direct reports would be desirable and undoubtedly beneficial.

And just as immediately, they remind me of their realities:

- Four *more* meetings a year? I don't have time to get done what I'm doing now!

In other words, you're so busy doing your job that you don't have time to add feedback to your responsibilities.

*WRONG!*

Feedback *IS* your job!

Whatever the specific details and responsibilities that accompany your position, your ability to provide — and receive — good, effective feedback, and to communicate the information feedback contains is the most important role you — or anyone — plays.

Most of the companies I work with have a 3:1 to 12:1 ratio of manager or supervisor to direct reports. If a manager spends most of his/her time making him/herself better, the company improves a little. If, however, the manager or supervisor spends quality time and gives good feedback to eight direct reports, and they perform consistently better, the company improves a lot.

THE MCLAUGHLIN MATRIX: *EVERYTHING IS ABOUT YOUR TEAM AND THE CONTRIBUTION THE TEAM MAKES TO THE BUSINESS.*

> *THE MORE QUALITY TIME YOU SPEND WITH YOUR DIRECT REPORTS, HELPING THEM DO THEIR JOBS, THE BETTER YOU BE-COME AT YOUR JOB.*
>
> Peter

Because they understand that feedback is their job, the managers not only provide a wider range of consistent benefits for their company, they also constantly contribute to the creation of a true feedback culture within the company.

Effective feedback cultures are created and sustained by individuals who know how feedback works, and the benefits it both provides and confers.

To return to the specific example above, effective feedback providers know how much such a quarterly schedule of feedback-related communication would change things — and change things for the better, from the inside, and from the bottom up.

In the course of teaching the principles of peak performance from my book CATCHFIRE to store managers and employees of the retail arm of clothing designer Polo/Ralph Lauren, I recommended that the company's regional managers have frequent conference calls involving five or so stores from different geographical areas to discuss the challenges they faced and, far more importantly, how other managers had *solved* problems.

The recommendation was acted upon, and the results were quite successful. The various managers began *learning* from one another, and at the same time they began *teaching* one another.

The phone conversations created a self-reinforcing feedback chain, and one of the reasons it worked so well was that each of its members was speaking the same language.

They understood one another's responsibilities and resources, as well as their challenges, and were able to *show* how they had approached similar problems in the Polo retail stores for which they were responsible.

The feedback chain took on a life of its own, with everyone providing and receiving feedback from everyone else.

This was a case of recommending that the people who know and understand what they are dealing with be put in contact with one another.

There's an important lesson here, and this is a good place to consider it:

Feedback works best when it's grounded in the real-world, *specific* nature of the job at hand.

The more specific, the better. And the more specific an understanding of circumstances and responsibilities and challenges that you show, the more appreciative the feedback's recipient will be.

By speaking the employee's or teammate's language, you remind that person of your organization's sense of community, and that he or she is a *part* of that community.

Polo/Ralph Lauren's store managers learned that lesson from one another — and you can bet that they, in turn, applied it when speaking with their salespeople.

*Once that regular communications link was established, the managers themselves developed a very effective internal feedback culture that suited themselves, their jobs, their work habits and patterns — and that produced large and ongoing benefits to the company.*

The managers had shown one another that they were part of something larger than their own day-to-day responsibilities.

- The more receptive you are to giving and getting feedback at work, the stronger network you create.
- Feedback improves business relationships. Effective, consistent feedback enables people to communicate more clearly and cogently on all levels. As a result, they learn more about one another.
- Recent research from the Gallup organization declares that the more team members know about one another personally, the greater the level of performance and teamwork productivity.
- Effective feedback creates fully engaged employees and better business results.

# FLATTERY ISN'T FEEDBACK — AND NEITHER IS NONSPECIFIC CRITICISM!

Effective feedback is always *honest* feedback.

*Always.*

The instant your sense of tact or company politics begin to temper, modify, or, worst case, *avoid* giving thorough, detailed, and honest feedback, you've compromised the feedback's effectiveness.

And there's the rub. Our culture in general and our business culture in specific present a number of barriers to the sorts of absolute honesty that good feedback requires.

We withhold truly honest feedback because we don't want to hurt feelings or we're not quite sure what the reaction to such feedback will be.

We're reluctant to offer feedback because we think being honest isn't always nice. But the truth is that when we don't give people honest feedback, we're keeping them in the dark, not allowing them to grow. We're not only not helping, we're actually harming the person's performance.

> "Lack of candor blocks smart ideas, fast action, and good people contributing all the stuff they've got. It's a killer."
> Jack Welch, former CEO of GE, author of *Winning*

It's not in anyone's best interest to hold back.

Here's an example we've all experienced:

Think about the time when someone came up to you saying that your blouse is unbuttoned or your zipper's down. Weren't you grateful they had the guts to tell you about the problem so that you could take care of it?

Now think about some of the familiar catchphrases and "good advice" that we hear throughout our lives:

- If you can't say something good, don't say anything at all.
- Don't rock the boat.
- Go along to get along.
- A spoonful of sugar helps the medicine go down.
- You catch more flies with honey than with vinegar.

I'm not saying that there's *no* good advice here. Tact is certainly a key social lubricant, and as we'll see shortly, truly effective feedback rests upon an absolute commitment to positive focus.

But there is a large difference between finding the right positive approach to delivering feedback, and delivering only constant good news and compliments that say nothing. Remember:

- "You're doing GREAT!" is a compliment, but it isn't feedback, even if it's true.
- "You're doing lousy!" isn't feedback either, even if it's true.

Part of the challenge, I believe, lies in that word *honesty*. While honesty is a cardinal virtue, it's a loaded word when it comes to feedback.

We've all seen — or, in some cases, suffered through! — movies or TV episodes where by some contrivance a character is rendered incapable of saying *anything* that isn't absolutely honest. If you've ever seen the Jim Carrey movie *LIAR LIAR*, you know exactly what I'm talking about:

"What a horrible dress you're wearing!"

"Yes, honey that dress does make your butt look fat!"

"That's the stupidest idea I've ever heard!"

And so on.

That's the sort of thing that makes for comedy (or what passes for it), but it isn't at all what we seek when we ground our feedback in honesty.

So let's keep the *concept* of honesty but look for a more useful term.

## CANDOR — CAN DO!

For Jack Welch, former CEO of GE, the term is *candor*.

And candor, according to Welch, is a quality almost as absent from most organizations as feedback itself. I understand why Welch prefers *candor* to *honesty* when it comes to describing. Candor is a more subtle word, and it gives more of a sense of the *quality* of information and comment (and feedback!) that Welch seeks in an organization.

Candor *includes* honesty but also embraces frankness and, by some definitions anyway, *impartiality*.

It's worth noting that the origins of *candid* are found in the Latin word *candere*, meaning to *shine*.

Feedback, presented candidly, does shine an honest, frank, and impartial light on its subjects. And one consequence of that light is that *things get done*. In terms of effective feedback, however, there is a word I prefer even to candor.

That word is:

REALISTIC!

# INTERLUDE

## EDGAR ALLAN POE AND SCOTT ADAMS (CREATOR OF DILBERT) UNCOVER THE ELEPHANT IN THE ROOM

I was in discussions recently with a small medical products company. We were speaking of potential projects, but I soon realized that nothing would go forward with the participants because they could not be candid with one another.

Edgar Allan Poe

As an outsider I could see the "elephant in the room" that the insiders refused to acknowledge.

Thoughts of that failed meeting carried me back to one of the first detective short stories ever written, which I had read in high school: "The Purloined Letter," by Edgar Allan Poe. ("Purloined," from Middle English, means "stolen.") The letter had been stolen from an unnamed woman's boudoir, to be used for blackmail purposes.

The Prefect of Police, who was having no luck finding the letter, called in amateur detective Auguste Dupin to help find it before embarrassing damage could be done. They had a suspect in mind and had searched his hotel room. The French police had looked behind the wallpaper, under the carpet, examined the furniture (with a microscope no less), and had no success.

The next day, Dupin, having found the missing letter in no time and with very little effort, presented it to the Prefect of Police. He explained to the Prefect that the thief was not only clever, he was also aware of standard police procedures. He knew that the police would look for an *elaborate* hiding place, and therefore he had hidden the letter in plain sight...

Dupin had found the letter precisely where no one had looked — in the letter box hanging on the wall, for anyone to see.

Many times, it is the amateur or the outsider who discovers the "elephant in the room" or in this case, the stolen letter sitting in plain sight in the "outgoing mail."

The Feedback Revolution is a new way for us all to become "amateur detectives" and become aware of what is all around us and nobody sees...until now.

Scott Adams, like Poe, uses a character to open the eyes of anyone paying attention. Adams used his years as a bank teller (among other jobs) to really understand what is going on in poorly run companies, and then reveals his thoughts through Dilbert and his assemblage of cartoon characters.

*Scott Adams, creator of Dilbert*

Mark Twain once remarked that HUMOR IS BASED ON GRIEVANCE; Dilbert brings most of the grievances we experience in our jobs and careers to light in sudden and stunning ways. He has a number of cartoons on feedback, which point out everything that's wrong and yet is still pervasive in most corporate cultures.

One cartoon has Dilbert returning a performance review nine months late and yet all he had done was sign what his direct report herself had written...he completes the second shot of the combination punch by adding that he didn't actually remember if he had even read it.

Another example shows him congratulating a worker for his good work yet telling the same person that he had given him "poor" in the write-up...in case he should ever have to fire him.

In yet a third cartoon panel, Dilbert talks of an employee "accused of unspecified shortcomings by a person who shall remain nameless." The accuser, of course, has been placed in a witness protection program adding to the absurdity of it all, which points to the reality.

The thing about actually seeing elephants in the room is that once they are discovered, we have to do something about them...or we'll have to clean up after them.

Once Dilbert alerts us that our company has no program for delivering and receiving candid and efficient feedback, we have to build one; then we have to train and reward those who practice it.

# GET REAL

*Realistic.* Nothing less than that.

Effective feedback is always grounded in an absolutely realistic understanding of the situation and circumstances being addressed.

Being realistic means that you and the feedback you offer are *always:*
- Specific
- Honest
- Candid
- Focused

That commitment to realism — without which you can have neither candor nor honesty — means that when offering feedback, you put away or free yourself from:
- Rose-colored glasses
- Best-case and worst-case projections
- Blue-sky hopes and ballpark figures
- Nonspecific "what ifs"
- Empty and information-free phrases

In other words, when preparing to offer feedback, you must put yourself in a realistic frame of mind and use that perspective to anchor the specific feedback you will be providing.

Here's a good way of looking at the difference between the sort of rose-colored, sugarcoated feedback that hobbles business effectiveness, and candid, specific, *realistic* feedback:

> **Courtier:** *His majesty is well turned-out today, though he perhaps might wish to consider adding a regal robe to his ensemble. Just in case the weather turns inclement.*
> **Honest Man:** *The Emperor is NAKED!*

Get the picture?

Thought so.

We'll be looking in more detail in later chapters at how you ensure that your feedback — and the feedback culture you're creating — remains relentlessly realistic. But there's another aspect of the realistic approach that's embedded in the commitment to realism, but might not be immediately obvious: *Timeliness.*

## TIMELINESS: UNLIKE FINE WINE, FEEDBACK DOES *NOT* GET BETTER WITH AGE

One vital aspect of being realistic is the inclusion of an awareness that the clock is always ticking.

Our business environments are constantly changing — and now are changing more quickly and more constantly than ever before.

• Effective feedback is *always* timely.

While fine wines improve with the passage of time, feedback doesn't.

• Feedback is a highly perishable commodity — undelivered feedback does no one any good. It's only good in the act of being presented and received — otherwise it's like wrapping a gift and not giving it.

Unfortunately, in many organizations, feedback is put on hold, generally until the date that a regularly scheduled review arrives.

Which could mean, theoretically at least, that a feedback point perceived the day after an employee's annual review might wait 364 days before being delivered.

By which point you and I — and the employee! — know pretty clearly how much that particular piece of feedback is worth. Think back to the Denver Broncos' Peyton Manning example from the first chapter...how much would feedback be worth if it was withheld until the end of the season, or even the end of the quarter? And yet we do it in the corporate world all the time.

> "I think having a very formal performance review process in an organization is an important thing, so I use that. The first time I did it, it worked well. I was very clear. I was able to use specific instances as examples. But I also learned that you can't wait many months after something happens for the formal review process to give

somebody feedback. So I started giving more immediate feedback, then revisited it in the formal review process."

Tiffany Cooper Gueye, chief executive of BELL

(Building Educated Leaders for Life), which assists urban children;

quoted by Adam Bryant in his "Corner Office" column,

The New York Times, September 11, 2011

And that's assuming that the point hasn't been forgotten in the time spent waiting for a formal review.

*Feedback won't wait — don't make it try to.*

A true feedback culture thrives on constant, timely feedback. It nurtures and nourishes that timeliness in various ways:

- Increased frequency of formal reviews
- Ongoing conversation and dialogue between managers and line reports, emphasizing feedback outside the constraints of formal review structures and procedures
- Open lines of communication that are always open
- The "habit" of feedback is deliberately cultivated — as is the fact that the habit demands timeliness

Speeding up the process of delivering effective feedback has a wonderful side effect that you might not have anticipated — although when it happens you'll wonder why you didn't see it coming:

*Faster feedback speeds everything up.*

Think about it.

If an organization's members are in constant communication, with feedback delivered in the most timely manner possible, *timeliness* itself becomes an ingrained habit.

That's because timely feedback is far more likely to be acted upon, and acted upon immediately, than feedback whose delivery has been delayed or deferred until the business's — or, even less excusably, the *manager's* — calendar "permits" it.

## FEEDBACK LOG: MARGIE

After numerous attempts to connect with a prospect in whom I'd invested a significant amount of time, I began convincing myself that she wasn't interested, that I had been used. But then a stroke of luck occurred — I bumped into her at a convention.

I politely asked her if there was something I had missed as I had been trying unsuccessfully to reach her via phone and email.

She replied that she'd been busy. I explained that my feelings were a little hurt. I thought our working relationship was progressing well, and I was under the impression that she had confidence in me and the services I could provide to her organization.

She agreed that we had a good relationship and that she was looking at her budget to partner with my organization. She then said she would be better at a follow-up with me in the future. Know what? She has kept her commitment. She is now a client!

The point — and it's one that I remind myself of constantly now — is that I could have made my feelings and my feedback known to her at the time I began to grow annoyed, rather than waiting for a chance encounter — which just as easily could not have happened.

*Margie*

Grounding feedback in the present doesn't mean that proper feedback can't serve medium- and long-term goals and targets — far from it. As we'll see later, effective feedback also *always* feeds forward.

But those goals and targets are best pursued — and achieved — when you start from a solid, grounded, and constantly reinforced understanding of *where you are now*.

In fact, no less an expert than Jack Welch has suggested that it can take more than a few quarters to establish an effective feedback culture within an organization.

Obviously, such a journey has to start somewhere.

And we know where that is.

> "At GE, it took us close to a decade to use candor as a matter of course, and it was by no means universal after twenty. Still it can be done. There is nothing scientific about the process. To get candor, you reward it, praise it, and talk about it. You make public heroes out of people who demonstrate it. Most of all, you yourself demonstrate it in an exuberant and even exaggerated way even when you're not the boss."
> Jack Welch, Winning

In order to introduce and develop a culture of feedback in your organization, you have to first understand what feedback is.

And in order to understand what feedback *is*, you need to experience it.

But at the moment, there's probably not a thorough and systematic approach to delivering and receiving feedback at your company; most companies are in the same boat. Before you can begin to deal with an elephant in the room, after all, you have to know that it's there, and you have to know that it's an elephant.

Here's the proper beginning place for confronting the feedback elephant: What sorts of so-called feedback have you experienced? What are the most common types of feedback — or what poses as feedback — in business today?

## FEEDBACK IS MORE THAN A PAYCHECK AND AN ANUUAL PERFORMANCE REVIEW

*"Your paycheck is feedback enough"* is a common-enough attitude in many businesses. People are getting paid — what more do they need?

- Salary isn't feedback — and neither are raises or bonuses. Compensation is a marker for performance, and an important one, but true *feedback* is more detailed and insightful than a number on a deposit slip. Paychecks have to be delivered — feedback can be put off.

*Your company has regularly scheduled feedback procedures, policies, and possibly even review/feedback software systems already in place* — why do you need more?

- You can answer that one yourself: How much do you, or any of your peers, direct reports, or superiors, look forward to those "regularly scheduled procedures"? More than that, there's likely to be constant avoidance of even ineffective, informal, approaches to feedback such as "standard checklist" performance reviews.

*You put off performance reviews* — and race through them when they can't be avoided any longer.

- Most reviews are menus of check-off items and box scores, delivered with as little dialogue as possible — and next to no true *conversation*.

*Your company's culture provides only negative feedback* — and that is generally given only when someone is screwing up.

- The most common type of feedback that employees receive at many companies is a chewing out when things have gotten bad enough that somebody has to say something.

*Your company walks away from feedback opportunities* — and does so constantly.

- Avoidance and denial are, of course, central to maintaining the delusion that there's no elephant in the room. Avoidance and denial are far easier to maintain than is the acknowledgment that there's an elephant in the room — and that somebody has to take care of it!

And those are just some examples of how feedback, as generally misunderstood, exists in many organizations.

# BUILDING A CATHEDRAL: EFFECTIVE FEEDBACK IS INCLUSIVE AND MOTIVATING

We're still a good distance from that overall feedback culture, from the transformation of our organizations into feedback factories, but our journey has begun.

Now let's look at how an employee's sense of his or her role within the larger organization and undertaking can radically improve the employee's sense of both work and self.

Don't stop me if you've heard this one before:

There's a story of the medieval knight who came across a group of stonemasons and other workers engaged in the early stages of a mammoth construction project. He asked the workers what they were doing; most responded by identifying their particular area of expertise: mixing mortar, shaping or setting stone, building frames and braces, and so on.

But one worker looked up with surprise when the question was asked of him. He hadn't even noticed the knight, so absorbed in his work was he.

With a huge grin, he puffed out his chest, pointed to himself, and said, "I'm building a cathedral!"

Admittedly, that's an old chestnut of tale, but oldies sometimes are indeed goodies, and the kernel of insight this story contains is particularly appropriate in terms of feedback:

*Someone* had given the enthusiastic worker good, effective feedback. Not just:

- Your mortar is well-mixed.
- Your bricks are well-placed.
- Your finished work meets our expectations.

But also, and above *all*:

- Your excellent work is an important part of the construction of a cathedral that will stand forever and be admired by all for its beauty and sturdiness.

By giving good feedback, you can help all of your employees get excited by their roles in the big picture. Which would you rather have: a team of bored cement makers and bricklayers, or a team of enthusiastic cathedral builders?

Now that we've laid the groundwork for what effective feedback is — and isn't — we're ready to begin putting it into practice, to start creating our feedback factory and feedback culture.

It's a challenging undertaking — but also an exciting one.

You could almost envision one of those 1960s-style call-to-action posters. This one would say:

**FEEDBACK NOW!!!!!!**

*Right on!*

## TIPS, TOOLS, & TACTICS

TIP: Feedback IS your business — whatever business you're in.

TIP: Unlike fine wine, feedback doesn't "keep" well.

TIP: Effective feedback is *always specific, realistic, and timely.*

TIP: Create a **FEEDBACK BOOKMARK** that pops up in your calendar or agenda on a regular but, if possible, unpredictable basis to remind you to offer someone a piece of effective feedback.

TOOL: Develop a *FEEDBACK PERSPECTIVE* — incorporate as much as possible into an ongoing conversation aimed at improving your company's performance and processes. View *everything* from a feedback perspective.

TOOL: Reward timely feedback, perhaps by setting up a feedback-on-feedback session to explore and share what it was that made the specific feedback effective, what its results and consequences were for the company, and so on. For example:

"This piece of feedback brought in additional revenue" — and then explain how the feedback produced that new revenue stream.

"This piece of feedback changed the way our company does things" — and then explore the feedback insights that produced the change.

"This piece of feedback was presented in a particularly creative way that increased its impact and effect" — and then show how it was creative and why creativity counts.

TOOL: Add the ability to give and receive effective feedback to every job description; this one-line change in a job description immediately makes feedback an HR as well as a management concern, and goes a long way toward laying the foundation for your Feedback Culture.

TOOL: Create and distribute an *I LOVE FEEDBACK* smiley-face button. (With a caveat that there's more to feedback than a button, but it's a good place to start.)

TACTIC: Honesty remains the best policy, but when delivering feedback, remember that honesty is only one aspect of *candor*. Be candid with your feedback, and encourage others to do the same.

TACTIC: Create a Feedback Log and stick to it, recording examples of feedback sessions, their outcomes, what went right, what needs improvement.

TACTIC: Make formal feedback a part of every monthly team meeting.

*Good moods enhance
the ability to think flexibly
and with more complexity,
thus making it easier to find
solutions to problems,
whether intellectual
or interpersonal.*

Daniel Goleman,
*Emotional Intelligence*

©Cartoonbank.com

*Keep up the good work, whatever it is, whoever you are.*

# CHAPTER THREE

# REAL. POSITIVE. FEEDBACK.

We've all had ineffectual managers or bosses like the one in the cartoon. Some of us have been that boss ourselves, at least occasionally.

While it's true that the manager in the cartoon is being positive, he's not being positive about anything *specific*. His words are as empty as his smile.

Let's look at how to use real substance to fill that cheerful void. To begin with, hang onto the positive attitude.

Effective feedback is *most* effective if it's positive.

That's completely different from saying that feedback itself is neither positive nor negative, isn't it? The athlete lives in a culture of feedback; a well-coached team is a feedback factory. That's what you want your company, your organization, your family to become.

What does such a feedback factory look like? Ask Dexter Fowler.

# ONE STEP AWAY

Dexter Fowler, center fielder for the Colorado Rockies, according to most experts is a step and a hit away from being among the best center fielders in baseball. How do you give the right kind of feedback to help him get to the next level?

Established superstars and future Hall of Famer Jason Giambi and Troy Tulowitzki solved the problem by asking him to join them in their off-season workouts. They didn't have to say "your first step is too slow" or "you're not physically strong enough" — they simply asked him to join them, two of the undisputed leaders in the Rockies' Clubhouse.

Dexter's results in the spring of 2012: seven pounds of muscle gained, body fat down 4%, and he has realized that it was strength at *his* core that would help him get that first step of quickness he needed to become a better base stealer; his batting average came up 30 points to over .300, and he was among the top six Major League hitters, with a 2012 on-base percentage of .393. The leadoff hitter, as the movie *Moneyball* reminded us, is the most important hitter on the team: What matters isn't the drama of the home run; it's getting players on base and working them around the diamond.

And as Dexter's story shows, sometimes the best feedback is *feedback by example*. You just have to make sure your employees or colleagues are ready to *receive* the feedback.

> Feedback need not always be communicated in words — put some creativity behind your thinking and turn feedback anxiety into positive anticipation.

To reach that goal — where your direct reports, for instance, approach feedback sessions in a state of receptivity, without trepidation — you have to guide them to the point where they, like the members of an athletic team, have come to understand that all feedback shouldn't fall into positive or negative categories.

And, paradoxically, one of the best ways to accomplish that is to make sure that your feedback is *always* presented in a positive way.

You cannot, in my opinion — and, fortunately for me, it's also the opinion of many scientists and psychologists — overestimate the importance of putting positive context on feedback, even when the feedback is addressing or presenting serious criticism or even termination.

Why?

Because positive *works*.

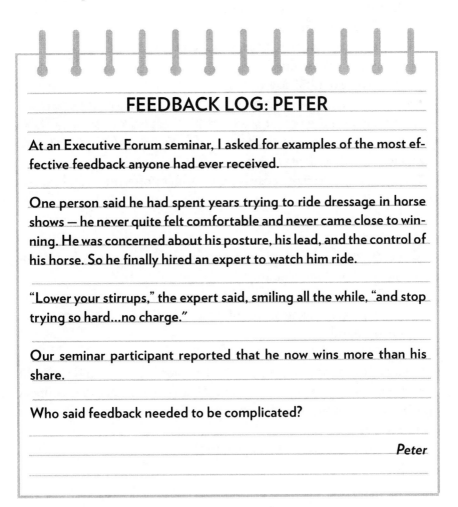

## FEEDBACK LOG: PETER

At an Executive Forum seminar, I asked for examples of the most effective feedback anyone had ever received.

One person said he had spent years trying to ride dressage in horse shows — he never quite felt comfortable and never came close to winning. He was concerned about his posture, his lead, and the control of his horse. So he finally hired an expert to watch him ride.

"Lower your stirrups," the expert said, smiling all the while, "and stop trying so hard...no charge."

Our seminar participant reported that he now wins more than his share.

Who said feedback needed to be complicated?

*Peter*

# POSITIVE DOESN'T MEAN "GOODY-GOODY" OR SUGARCOATED

Before we get to what I mean when I use the word "positive" in a feedback context, let's take a moment to look at what I *don't* mean.

When I say "positive," I'm not talking about:

- Unrealistic expectations or observations
- Goody-goody approaches to anything
- Blindly optimistic attitudes toward performance
- Sugary-sweet *anything*
- Avoidance of unpleasant topics

And guess what? The great pioneers of positive attitudes weren't advocating any of those postures either! We'll get back to some of those pioneers in a moment, but since I've told you what "positive" isn't, let's take a look at what I believe it *is*.

The truly and *effectively* positive approach to offering — and receiving — feedback is:

- Realistic
- Honest
- Detailed and specific — even when the specific details are unpleasant or disconcerting
- Careful to include affirmative observations and comments even when presenting negative information or sharp criticism
- Encouraging
- Nonjudgmental

Not a Pollyanna wearing a pair of rose-colored glasses in the bunch!

And not a single aspect or element that prevents or even hampers you from presenting specific criticism or less than "positive" performance reviews.

It's all a matter of how you approach things.

## POSITIVELY SELIGMAN AND PETERSON

For much of the history of psychological research and diagnosis, the emphasis was on what was *wrong* — maladies, disorders, syndromes, malfunctions, and diseases. This was important and in many cases critical information and knowledge, but most of it focused on recognizing, identifying, and diagnosing problems, to understand the many things that could go wrong in the mind.

The standard text, in fact, was called the *Diagnostic and Statistical Manual of Mental Disorders* (first edition 1952, and in print continuously since then). The DSM remains a standard text.

Standard and in many ways comprehensive — but in one crucial area incomplete.

What was missing was a concerted scientific effort to identify what could go right.

That gap began to be filled by the work of Martin Seligman, Ph.D, and the late Christopher Peterson, Ph.D, who undertook a mammoth research and investigative project aimed at identifying the positive qualities of mind and character that have been consistent — and consistently effective — throughout human history.

Their work, which traced a path back to the civilizations of Greece and Rome, was called Character Strengths and Virtues. It was published in 2004 and provided a practical framework for identifying aspects of positive psychology — a framework that has had a great effect.

The qualities and virtues Seligman and Peterson identified as central to positive psychology are:

- WISDOM AND KNOWLEDGE
- COURAGE
- HUMANITY
- JUSTICE
- TEMPERANCE
- TRANSCENDENCE

> These qualities and virtues, and the numerous positive characteristics (and the 24 Signature Strengths that flow from these six virtues) that comprise them, are at the heart of wellbeing, of a life well-lived. They are qualities and virtues that have much to offer to business as well as all other walks of life.
>
> They are, it should be clear, valuable qualities to bring to your feedback as well.
>
> By their work and its documentation, Seligman and Peterson showed that "positivity" isn't simply a "feel-good" word, but a proven human quality that can be developed, and one of the most important that we possess.

I learned *my* lessons in various ways, but one of the key lessons came to me at the top of a flight of stairs I'd climbed hundreds, perhaps thousands, of times.

## THE MIRROR AT THE TOP OF THE STAIRS — FINDING YOUR FEEDBACK ZONE

At one time my consulting firm was on the second floor of an office building. I usually took the stairs and generally used my climb to arrange my thoughts and prepare myself for whatever needed to be discussed with my team.

It was a routine, and one that I was accustomed to and that, I thought, served me well and, in turn, did the same for my team.

At the top of the flight of stairs was a full-length mirror, and to this day I don't know why it was there. As with the stairs, I had encountered that mirror countless times.

This particular day, however, it wasn't the mirror I noticed when I finished my climb — it was *me*.

My shoulders were slumped, my eyes cast down, my general demeanor one that spoke of many things — none of them positive.

I felt in some ways as though I were seeing myself for the first time, and for a moment I really disliked what I saw.

My demeanor displayed everything I was against, even though I had researched the effects of physical bearing and positive emotion on performance. As I would later write in CATCHFIRE:

*You can't be a winner if you walk like a loser.*

*How*, I wondered, *can I expect to manage anyone, much less lead them, when this is what they see? No matter how good the messages I have to share, this particular messenger will affect outcomes simply by his appearance.*

But in the next moment I realized that even that bit of feedback I'd given myself was, like my posture, slumped over, downcast.

I decided to try something different. Instead of castigating myself for how I *had been* appearing, I would change the way I *do appear*. I replaced a negative with a positive.

To use some psychological terms that we'll be exploring in more detail, I replaced my

- **Negative Explanatory Style** — *(the way you explain mistakes you've made) past-looking, focused on failure or, if not outright failure, on what I was doing "wrong"*

with a

- **Positive Explanatory Style** — *forward-facing, focused on effectiveness, aware of how I can do things "right"*

I don't know if my team noticed the change in me that morning — I suspect they did — but I am certain that I noticed it.

In fact, that mirror became as central to my routine as the stairs that led to it.

And it didn't take me long to realize that routine was the wrong word for what I was doing.

I had created a *ritual* for myself, one that reinforced itself — and me — by incorporating a quick but thorough self-inspection into my preparations for situations where others would be, among many things, inspecting me.

Ritual, you see, plays a large role in all our lives, not simply the ceremonial aspects — worship, weddings, funerals — of every part of our lives.

Once we're aware of that role, we can begin actively using ritual in new and exciting ways, not the least of them the way we provide feedback.

> "When you do something...the quality of your state of mind is the activity itself. When you are concentrated on the quality of your being, you are prepared for the activity."
>
> Zen Master Shunryu Suzuki

# THE PRE-FEEDBACK RITUAL

Why am I talking about ritual now?

Because preparing ourselves to give effective feedback can be as important as the feedback itself.

And ritual can be an important part of that preparation.

I'm not talking about elaborate rituals, you understand. My pause before that full-length mirror took only a few seconds, yet it reset my sense of myself and, more importantly, established the tone and demeanor I wished to present to everyone in the office. The glance at the mirror became a ritual of preparation.

We see examples of small rituals constantly in sports:

- The baseball player who swings the weighted bat while waiting in the on-deck circle — he's not only loosening himself up physically, he's getting his mind and emotions ready for his stand at the plate.
- Tiger Woods, who follows a precise, identical procedure every time he prepares to putt.
- Symphony orchestras have a ritual in which, after the rest of the orchestra is seated, the first violinist plays an A note, to which all others tune. The ritual calms and alerts the orchestra that the performance is about to begin.
- The great French novelist Georges Simenon was legendary for his productivity, turning out hundreds of novels over his career. Before beginning a book, he would have a physical examination to ensure that his progress wouldn't be interrupted by illness; then he would block out nine days on his calendar, stuff several pipes, sharpen his pencils, and begin.

✧ On the other hand, Isaac Asimov, who wrote as many books as Simenon, but on a far wider variety of subjects, insisted that his own ritual was simple as could be: he insisted only that his typewriter be turned on and that he was seated at the proper distance for his fingers to reach the keyboard.

As I pointed out in CATCHFIRE, the best rituals energize, calm, and focus us — a powerful and very *positive* combination.

In each case, the athlete or musician or writer is performing a personal act that has the effect of reminding him or her of the job at hand, refocusing his attention and centering himself in the present.

*Preparation to deliver effective feedback requires both content preparation and emotional preparation.*

Ritual can provide similar benefits for you as you prepare to provide feedback to your employees or direct reports.

On the other hand, lack of emotional and physical preparation can sabotage even the most carefully considered and documented feedback.

Which would *you* prefer to experience:

- A review in which your superior fumbles for notes, searches for words, gives every impression of just wanting to *get the thing over with* — *even if the bulk of the review is positive.*
- A review in which your superior is confident, organized, and prepared in every way.

Now ask yourself which experience your team would most appreciate receiving from you.

Obviously, those are loaded examples. Yet we've all been through reviews or similar business conversations that were less feedback conversations than they were "necessary evils" that the reviewer sought to get through as quickly as possible.

If we're honest, we've probably been responsible for some of those low-value conversations ourselves.

We can avoid those situations, and vastly increase the value and content of our feedback sessions, by committing to a brief preparation ritual before the session begins.

The rituals I have discussed here are mine and have worked for me. I believe that they will work for you, but I also know that you must make them your own, adapting and adjusting them to suit your nature and your style of work and interaction with yourself and with others.

*Find your own most effective ritual and use it* — although I would recommend that it include a bit of physical movement or exercise for the psychological/emotional benefits it provides.

What matters most, though, is that we "pause before that mirror" to put ourselves in the right and most effective frame of mind before entering the room.

Whether your "pre-feedback ritual" consists of
- Deep breathing exercises in your office
- Meditating for three minutes
- Doing a stretching exercise
- Going for a brisk walk and letting your unconscious work

The point is that you are deliberately cultivating the habit of preparing for the feedback session ahead.

And what you are really doing is making sure that the feedback session will be a positive experience for all involved.

You are, in other words:
- Taking action *before* the feedback session commences
- Putting on your *own* oxygen mask before you help others

And, as pioneering psychologist Martin Seligman has shown, the best way to be positive is through action. You can't get there just by thinking positive thoughts. Seligman should know — he is, after all, considered to be the father of positive psychology.

Which brings us to the key question:
- Why be positive?

And the key answer:
- Because even in dire or disastrous situations, *positive works!*

# FEEDBACK LOG: PETER

I was part of a group of 100 entrepreneurial leaders and visionaries, including management expert Peter Drucker, in Tarrytown, NY. We heard a presentation by a CEO, a crisis manager who was put in charge of an electronics business, one of the leading companies of Stockholm, Sweden.

I asked him afterward how he gave feedback to people whose jobs he had to change, downgrade, or eliminate. He said he was at his best (calm, focused, and energized) in the early evening, so when he had the toughest feedback to give, including letting people go, he would conduct the meeting over dinner.

It got to be a joke around the company. Don't accept a dinner invite from the boss.

Seriously, though, his theory about delivering tough feedback:

- Pick a time and place when you're emotionally calm

- Bad news is best delivered face to face

- Spend time preparing both content and context

*Peter*

# INTERLUDE

## MARTIN SELIGMAN –
## POSITIVE PSYCHOLOGY VERSUS THE SMILEY BUTTON

**M**artin Seligman, author of *Authentic Happiness*, tells the story about his daughter, who was five at the time and was working with him in the garden. She was dancing around and throwing the weeds and cuttings into the air when he yelled at her to stop disrupting his work.

She answered his complaint with direct and timely feedback. She said that after being told over a year ago that she was a complainer, she

*Martin Seligman*

had stopped complaining, at least most of the time. If she could stop complaining about everything, she said, then why can't he stop being "such a grouch."

Seligman, a Ph.D psychologist at the University of Pennsylvania, was also president of the American Psychological Association. This "feedback episode" started him thinking about his life as a father and as a researcher and teacher. Why was he such a grouch? Instead of being angry about her "work habits," he should be helping his daughter build up her strengths and encouraging her to achieve as much happiness as possible.

This epiphany, along with other insights, led him to put forth a call for psychology and psychologists to begin to generate as much focus on strengths and positive emotions, and as much interest in building the best things in life as in repairing the worst. Help people go from "languishing" to "flourishing."

This was the "birth" of positive psychology...evidence-based research on the role of positive emotions in helping us build our lives to be the best we can be, with more happiness and meaning.

The outcomes of this research form a baseline for great feedback. The end goal is always to help people perform better, build better relationships, and be better teammates. Even tough feedback, though structured in a straightforward and candid way, should come from as positive a stance as possible.

Nicki, Seligman's daughter, had given her father candid feedback, and it was the kindling to start the fire for a major advancement in psychology.

My acquaintance with Seligman goes back to his book *Learned Optimism* and his work with MetLife Insurance, with three years of practical research proving that optimistic insurance salespeople outsell less optimistic ones by 21% to 57%, and, even better, that people can learn to be optimistic.

## A SMILEY-FACED YELLOW BUTTON IS NOT ENOUGH

Lest you think Seligman and other positive psychologists wear their smiley buttons, read *The Secret*, and attend New Age meetings, think again. These people are some of the best, most mentioned, most serious researchers around. But they also know how to reach out to share their findings with the general public as well as their academic peers. On addition to frequent appearances in scholarly journals, Seligman and other positive psychologist are also often quoted in *The Wall Street Journal, Time, The New York Times,* and *Harvard Business Review.* They are able to show their research into such topics as "positive environments and the bottom line" and the role of gratitude in building an efficiently functioning corporate culture.

The lesson of being of a positive, optimistic mindset as a prelude to delivering feedback or opening a meeting for an annual review is key for improvement within corporate teams — or, for that matter, in school or at home.

# FIND YOUR FEEDBACK ZONE

In telling the story of the Swedish CEO at this point, I deliberately chose an example involving negative feedback.

The CEO's presentation of that feedback is a good reminder that a positive approach can be made central to otherwise negative situations and contexts. But it's a reminder of more than that. (So good was he that most of the 50 execs he was forced to let go or "help into other businesses" are still his friends.)

By establishing a formal pattern for the delivery of bad news — a dinner — and placing at the center of the pattern his own accurate sense of himself, he was at his best in the evenings; the CEO established a ritual, one based on finding his own most effective Feedback Zone.

In *CATCHFIRE* I characterized this Zone as one consisting of:
- ENERGY
- CONFIDENCE
- CALMNESS

That remains a good characterization, and I hope you find it helpful.

Finding your own Feedback Zone is an essential part of delivering effective feedback. If we're distracted, nervous, anxious, we're out of our Zone. If we're focused, confident, positive, appreciative, we're in our Zone, even when bad news must be delivered.

Look again at my log of the Swedish CEO's efforts in this area. We can see that he prepared for the feedback session by addressing, deliberately and ritually, the three main components of finding your Zone:
- Energy: For the CEO, his most effective energy levels arrived in the evening
- Attitude: He remained calm and positive
- Environment: By setting his feedback sessions at a dinner, the CEO humanized the delivery of unfortunate news

These elements will be different for each of us and will be chosen to suit our temperaments, natures, and budgets. Not all of us have the wherewithal to choose a four- or five-star restaurant for feedback sessions!

Perhaps your highest energy levels and best ability to remain calm arrive in the morning.

For myself, physical exercise is key to remaining in my Feedback Zone.

You might prefer to present bad news — or, for that matter, good news — in a nicely appointed office or in a spot removed from the workplace.

By examining yourself and your nature, you'll discover where your Feedback Zone lies, what its central elements are, and how to use pre-feedback ritual to ensure that you are there.

Now let's look at how to make sure that your feedback — and your approach to it — remains positive.

> "Companies with better than a 2.9:1 ratio for positive to negative statements are flourishing. Below that ratio, companies are not doing well economically."
>
> Barbara Fredrickson, Ph.D, author, *Positivity*

# FOSTERING GRATITUDE, THE "MOTHER OF ALL VIRTUES"

You will find, probably quickly, that establishing a positive approach in one area of your work — delivering feedback — spreads to other areas of both work and life.

There's good scientific evidence of this, found in the work of psychologist Barbara Frederickson, whose "Broaden and Build" theory has shown that positive psychology — maintaining a positive emotional outlook and demeanor — results in enhanced creativity, problem-solving, and the ability to comprehend and tackle large projects.

But how do you find and maintain that positive approach?

For myself, as I've mentioned, regular exercise is vital. In addition to the well-known benefits of an exercise session — cardiovascular and neurochemical benefits — the inclusion of exercise in my feedback ritual serves to put me in my Feedback Zone even before I've showered and dressed after a workout.

An acquaintance of mine took an approach that I find fascinating and recommend:

In order to remind himself of the importance of the positive, my acquaintance resolved to perform at least one conscious act of gratitude every day.

Whether it was:

- A handwritten thank-you note to someone who would not be expecting it
- A genuinely appreciative conversation with a person whose duties are too often overlooked — a retail checkout clerk, for instance
- Performing a good deed
- Contacting a friend to thank him or her for a long-forgotten act

The emphasis is on act of gratitude, by the way. He required that he take action in order to fulfill his daily quota of gratitude.

It wasn't always easy. Among the rules he set for himself was that the act must not be perfunctory.

(Saying "Thanks a lot" instead of just "Thanks" didn't count.)

And no matter how little he might feel like offering appreciation for anything on some days, his rule was inflexible. He had to write that unexpected thank-you note, make that unsolicited phone call, and make sure that they were sincere, and make sure that they involved taking action.

He found that the positive attitude created by this daily ritual began to spread throughout his life. Most days he now performs far more than a single act of gratitude. His sense of appreciation deepened, and he became a better and far more effective communicator of feedback:

- The more you practice gratitude, the more you see to be grateful for:
  ◇ GRATITUDE FOSTERS OPTIMISM!

There's more than one lesson for us here. While the key lesson is the importance of appreciation in establishing a positive psychological approach, there's a lesson in ritual here as well:

Among the rules for his daily expression of appreciation was that the thanks must be:

◇ Genuine

◇ Thoughtful

◇ Personal

In other words, there was *nothing* perfunctory about the appreciations he expressed.

And in the same way, there is never anything perfunctory about the delivery of effective feedback, whether the feedback contains good news or bad.

## POSITIVE COMES FIRST

Michael Nelson, EdD, Professor Emeritus at University of Kentucky and co-author of the leading textbook on teaching children with emotional disorders, has had a unique perspective on feedback. Although his textbook has long focused on proven evidence-based methods for teaching these children to manage their troublesome classroom behaviors, he and his colleagues have more recently begun to focus on preventing these behaviors before they take hold.

Their approach, Positive Behavioral Intervention and Support (PBIS), helps teachers in the early grades organize their classrooms to better foster adaptive social behaviors in all children in the class. In the past, a child who misbehaved would often receive nothing but negative feedback from a teacher: "Stop talking," "Don't interrupt," "Get back in your seat," "Can't you do anything right?!"

In the PBIS approach, at the beginning of the school year, teachers post a short list of positive behaviors at the front of the classroom such as "Be Safe," "Be Respectful," and "Be Prepared." Each has several examples such as "Walk, don't run, in classrooms or hallways" (Be Safe); "Wait your turn to ask questions or make a comment" (Be Respectful); and "Have your pencil, paper, or books ready to go at the beginning of each period" (Be Prepared). These are discussed with the entire class so that each child understands these positive expectations.

In this way, when a teacher sees the beginning of even minor instances of misbehavior, he or she can simply-say quietly to the classroom, "Remember, we all need to be respectful," and then perhaps follow up with a positive prompt to the child who is misbehaving: "Johnny, are you waiting your turn?" In this way, these positive instances of feedback not only help to set a positive norm for everyone in the classroom but also provide specific assistance to students at risk of misbehavior by teaching them positive behaviors with their potential misbehaviors.

Several randomized, controlled trials on such school-wide positive behavioral support have now begun to show reductions in front-office discipline referrals and even increases in school test scores.

## POSITIVES OUTNUMBER NEGATIVES IN EFFECTIVE FEEDBACK

Having just said so much about not being perfunctory, I'm now going to give you a formula that may at first appear perfunctory but that, if properly approached, is anything but:

- Make an effort to ensure that you deliver an AT LEAST 3:1 positive to negative ratio of feedback, even in highly critical (in the negative performance sense) situations. This is always a good rule of thumb, but if you must deliver bad news that is not the employee's "fault" — e.g., downsizing — this rationale becomes even more critical in the tough times.

It's not that hard, really. Here's what you do:

For every negative feedback you have to give (such as "You need to improve on hitting your deadlines," or "The team needs more input from you," or "Some of the team members are telling me you're too abrasive with them") balance it out by offering at least three pieces of positive feedback. You can offer four or five if you want to. But at a bare minimum, you need to stick to at least three positives for every negative.

Here's a good example of addressing a problem with an employee, and doing so in a positive manner:

"Your insights are valuable, and the team really looks up to you because of what you bring to the table. The team needs you — and we really need you to get those insights to us in a more timely manner. What do you think the best way of addressing this is?"

You want your direct report to improve his or her performance, productivity, work habits, whatever. And you want to energize them so that they will want to improve. The last thing you want is for them to walk out of your office feeling deflated and defeated. Remember, part of your job is to orchestrate the energies of the people around you. By tempering each negative with at least three positives, you'll succeed in keeping your direct reports motivated and upbeat. This piece of evidence-based advice forces you to think through each one of your direct reports or team members, or kids. Some days it's difficult to think of three or more positive traits — but if you keep at it, you will find some that you never noticed or thought of before. Looking for the positive gives you whole new ways of seeing your people!

My suggestion is that you start and end with a positive, but it has to be honest. Maybe start with two areas where this person has really done a good job. Talk about how much you and the company appreciate what they did. Talk about how much the team has benefited thanks to them.

After you've talked about a couple of positives, bring in the negative. Talk about areas of concern, always with specifics. Go over it thoroughly, make sure they understand it, and then move on. No need to belabor the point. Once they've got it, continue. (The 20/80 rule applies here: Spend 20% of time on the problem, get it out of the way, then spend 80% on moving forward.)

Try to end with what I call "a positive emotional wake." This way, you lift the energy back up, and the person walks out of your office on an upbeat note. Remember, you have to share everything — the good, the bad, the ugly — but you don't have to be insensitive about it. Keep that energy level up. Have empathy for your direct report. Deliver with compassion, sensitivity, and tact. Stick to a 3:1 (or better) positivity ratio.

Almost as good as the results you'll see flowing from this approach is the fact that it's based on solid, tested science.

In fact, let's take a look at the science now.

## FEEDBACK LOG: MARGIE

I was living in Heidelberg, Germany, and working for the US Army 7th Medical Command.

My boss, a civilian, was a risk-averse manager who always seemed to stay just under the radar, and did so by way of relentless mediocrity.

Nothing bad and nothing great ever came out of our office. *Ever.*

On one particular project, I had a great idea and plan that would showcase our office and provide a new opportunity for our mission and objectives. He asked me to work up a plan, which I did, and upon the "ta-da" and presentation of the plan, his only reply was...

...and what will you do next month, Mrs. Mauldin...?

He didn't want to raise the bar and future expectations for our work — he was quite content to be mediocre...and to have his feedback be the same.

How different things would have been if he had taken even a modestly positive approach.

My own feedback for him?

I started looking for another job the next week.

Margie

# PUTTING MORE POSITIVES THAN NEGATIVES INTO EVEN THE TOUGHEST FEEDBACK PRODUCES RESULTS!

The more I studied in the new field of positive psychology, the more I became increasingly aware that the study of positivity was a dynamic and lively field. Of course, like any such area of scientific inquiry, the dynamism and liveliness were matched from time to time by controversy and dispute. Feedback -- often spirited -- is, after all, the essence of the scientific method. Papers and findings are presented, and then are challenged and rebutted by other scientists.

One such case involved a fascinating study called "Positive Affect And The Complex Dynamics Of Human Flourishing," conducted by professors Barbara L. Fredrickson, then of the University of Michigan, and Marcial F. Losada of the Universidade Católica de Brasília in Brazil. Fredrickson had already developed a theory on positive emotions, while Losada had developed what appeared to be a model of team performance. Putting these two models together and conducting further research, they probed two key questions:

- "What predicts whether people will flourish or languish?"
- "Are the predictors similar for individuals, relationships, and larger groups?"

As it turned out, flaws in Losada's methodology prompted Frederickson to withdraw the parts of the paper related to his research. Now, *that's* feedback in action!

But the core of Frederickson's work and thought remain sound. Her insights are striking, and are increasingly widely accepted.

Basically, those insights say that when the number of positives exceeds the number of negatives at a certain level, the result is an individual -- or, by extension, a team, company, culture—who is *flourishing*. In this context, *flourishing* means to "live within an optimal range of human functioning, one that connotes goodness, generativity, growth, and resilience." By the way, generativity means a concern for people beyond yourself and your immediate family. In other words, genuinely caring about your fellow human.

Any of us who work with other people—or, for that matter, have a family—can see that keeping the number of positives well above the number of negatives delivers beneficial results.

In other words, when you add up all the positive stuff that goes on in a person—feeling grateful and upbeat, for example, liking others, liking themselves—and then add up all the negative stuff (like being irritable, disliking people or events, feeling contemptuous), then the ratio of the number of "good" things to the number of "bad" things, over time, needs to lean heavily toward the positive.

OK, in plain English: On average, over time, you need to be feeling and acting good about yourself, others, and life at least three times, in my opinion, more often than you're feeling crummy about things, in order to flourish.

You don't need a complex mathematical formula to see that this applies to individuals and groups, in both private and social contexts. Which means that it applies to your direct reports and to your team as a whole. So for a team to be performing well, it needs to express, experience, or receive a *noticeably* higher number of positives for every negative.

Remember, my *noticeably higher* number is a *general* conclusion, not a precise or quantifiable formula. The point is that when you have positives outnumbering negative by a ratio that the team is able to perceive, the benefits begin to flow. Go below a noticeable number to the point where there are about the same number of positives as negatives, and performance drops. Self-perception diminishes. People start to feel unhappy, dissatisfied, hollow, empty. Not something you want for your team. Or anyone, for that matter.

Even without the math, I believe that Frederickson would say that, in general, taking positives even higher than, for example, 3-1 is likely to be beneficial.

You can see it in your own life. If you're experiencing, say, five positives for every negative, you're going to feel better. And the better you feel, the better it is for your overall health—mind, body, and spirit.

Now think about this would affect a group such as your team. When there is a sharply noticeable number of positives over negatives, the benefits to a person or group include:

- Wider attention span
- Increased creativity

- Improved immune function
- Greater resilience to adversity
- Increased happiness
- Less affected by stress

Keeping this in mind as you shape the feedback you are going to deliver will not only deliver those benefits, it will also put the negatives which are being addressed into sharper focus, enabling the recipients to correct them efficiently—and positively.

As the following box shows, you don't *need* a precise statistical formula for that!

---

### AVOIDING THE "FEEDBACK SANDWICH" EVEN IN TOUGH DIALOGUES

I want to say again that my recommendation of a noticeable ratio of positives over negatives is not intended to be a precise formula or recipe. You're not making a "feedback sandwich" or calculating an accounting spreadsheet. Your feedback and the ratio of positive to negative it contains is a lively human activity, not a mechanical exercise, and must feel that way to the recipients.

---

## PRACTICALLY POSITIVE

Even our quick tour of the cutting-edge science behind the positivity ratio should remind you that there's more to this than just making a list of three or four positive things to remember to say when your job calls on you to deliver the news that someone's is being eliminated. That's why I warned earlier about perfunctory approaches to the positivity ratio, and that's why I'm repeating the reminder now.

It's hard to imagine a better example of "perfunctory positivity" than that manager in the cartoon back at the beginning of this chapter. He's saying nothing to his team—and even less to himself.

But when you take a deep and serious approach to building that positivity ratio, you are definitely talking with yourself as well as with your direct reports.

What you are doing is reminding yourself that all feedback works best when cast in a positive attitude.

The Swedish CEO who invites recipients of bad news to talk over a meal insists that his delivery of the news be accompanied by an exploration of as many honest positives as he can enumerate.

Your most effective feedback will do the same.

Suppose you have a direct report whose thoroughness in filing required information has begun to slip, even as her performance on the rest of her job continues to be strong.

The traditional approach—in the manner of those all-yelling-all-the-time coaches from the first chapter—would be to say something (or send a memo or email) to the effect of:

- Get your act together and file the reports on time and in proper format. Now!

And, probably, her reports would become more timely and complete—for a while. At which point you'd say or send the same message. When the great UCLA coach John Wooden wrote about feedback, he made the following point:

> "Approval is a greater motivator than disapproval, but we have to disapprove on occasion when we correct. It's necessary. I make corrections only after I have proved to the individual that I highly value him. If they know we care for them, our correction won't be seen as judgmental. I also try to never make it personal."

Now *that's*

   REAL

      POSITIVE

         FEEDBACK

# TIPS, TOOLS, & TACTICS

TIP: Feedback is always most effective when it's positive.

TIP: Positive doesn't mean rose-colored or sugar-coated.

TIP: At the outset of your feedback session, you'll need more practice; the *MORE* feedback you give, the better you'll be at it.

TOOL: Maintain at least a 3:1 positive to negative feedback ratio.

TOOL: Put on your own oxygen mask first. Being in a positive state of mind is essential for giving feedback, even with some negative content.

TOOL: Use a feedback checklist form as part of your feedback ritual, to write notes as you're preparing for feedback.

TACTIC: Begin and end feedback sessions with positives, helping ensure that the recipients enter and depart the session in as positive a frame of mind as possible.

TACTIC: Start out by asking permission to give them feedback. It lends a powerful psychological framework for their acceptance.

TACTIC: No matter how the session went, always thank the participants at the end. The story goes that no matter how tense a meeting, or what its outcome, Ronald Reagan always told a joke, or had someone else tell one, at the conclusion. Not by accident was, and is, Ronald Reagan referred to as "The Great Communicator."

*You cannot speak of ocean to a well-frog,*
*the creature of a narrower sphere.*
*You cannot speak of ice to a summer insect,*
*the creature of a season.*

Chuang Tzu

# CHAPTER FOUR

# THIS IS YOUR BRAIN ON FEEDBACK

In giving and receiving feedback, it helps if all parties are on the same page.

It helps even more if all the pages are in the same language.

## LOST IN TRANSLATION

For years I was perplexed by my inability to close certain deals.

These weren't troubled sales calls or botched negotiations. They were good calls I had put a lot of work and energy into.

Proposals, conversations, and follow-up meetings all went well — and often went far better than well. I didn't have to sense the enthusiasm on the part of the prospects — they *told* me how much they enjoyed and appreciated my work. Clearly we were all on the same page.

And then — no sale.

What went wrong?

More to the point: What was I doing wrong?

I decided to find out — and to do so by giving *myself* feedback on any of my unsuccessful sales.

I performed my pre-feedback ritual, found my Feedback Zone, reminded myself to be specific, and began my review, focusing on my own performance. Only gradually did it occur to me to broaden my horizon and to look at the variety of prospective clients who'd declined to commit to my services.

My proposals, fees, and negotiations were the same for them as for others who had signed on with me. What set my performance with the prospects who turned me down apart from those who signed on with me?

Answer: *Nothing.*

And that was the problem.

As I reviewed my own performance, I noticed that the prospects who most consistently turned me down fell into several broad categories:

- Engineering Firms
- Manufacturers
- Scientific Companies
- Financial Services

Notice anything in common among those categories?

If you paid attention to the cartoon at the beginning of this chapter, you're probably well ahead of me.

To use some terms that have been around for a while, and that you are at least slightly familiar with, I was caught in a right-brain/left-brain paradox.

The firms that most consistently turned me down were companies involved in businesses and industries that had certain similar orientations:

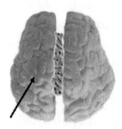

- Mathematical
- Logical
- Literal
- Precise
- Detail-oriented

*Left Hemisphere*

In other words, companies that were built upon, valued, and used left-brain skills and capabilities in their business. I'm a right-brain person:

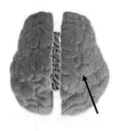

- Imaginative
- Intuitive About Ideas
- "Big Picture" Improvisational
- Enjoys the Unusual
- Socially Aware

*Right Hemisphere*

My prospects seemed to appreciate what I proposed in terms of content and ideas. But when the call for commitment came, their analytical left-brain assessments of me and my right-brain proposal said, "No."

I lost a lot of money speaking the wrong language to the right prospects — speaking, in fact, right-brain language to left-brain customers. That's too simple an explanation, as I'll soon show you.

And the feedback I gave myself?

I understood that I was unlikely to overturn my own nature; and to be frank, I didn't want to. I like who I am, and on the whole I do well with being myself.

But I wanted to land some of that left-brain-oriented business because there was a lot of it and they seemed to pay their bills on time.

My feedback session with myself gave me an idea of how to do it.

When presenting to left-brain prospects, I worked hard to be more organized, use far more specific terminology, temper my improvisation with practical and *practiced* analytical detail, and so on.

In short, I began to give left-brain presentations to my left-brain audience.

And once I began speaking *their* language, they began hearing mine, and I began landing their business. (As a matter of fact, 60% of my current business comes from left-brain-style organizations.)

We were always on the same page — I just had to make sure each of our pages was in the same language.

# TYPECASTING

Understanding whom you're giving feedback to is as vital as the nature of the feedback itself.

A world-class sales professional who loathes detailed micromanagement is unlikely to respond well to a multi-page point-by-point review of her work.

Conversely, a checklist-focused, detail-oriented precisionist is probably not going to take seriously a feedback session that is overly relaxed and informal.

## FEEDBACK LOG: PETER

The top brass at IBM Global Services was in planning mode, mapping out strategies for the competitive environment they faced and the services they would provide. Their teams were tasked with putting together reports and providing the information — the feedback — needed to ensure that the strategies were realistic.

More than once the teams presented large, richly and minutely detailed proposals, supported by stacks of equally detailed material — and each time the top brass reacted with what appeared to be boredom.

Eventually the team members came to realize that the response they were receiving wasn't simply boredom.

It was overload!

It was: "Oh no, not more pages!"

It was also, unfortunately, not clearly expressed — the team could have used better feedback.

But even without the feedback being directly given, the team members recognized that the thinking styles demanded by their work — detail-oriented, tactical plans — were not the thinking styles demanded by the top brass. They were "big picture" thinkers, and the plans they were making were "big picture" plans.

They trusted their teams to know the details — what they needed was a broader view that would help them formulate the strategies that their teams would turn into tactical action and accomplishment.

— Peter

Want a more fanciful example? Imagine Woody Allen, for instance, giving direction to Ayn Rand! Or Oprah offering feedback to Donald Trump!

Problems?

No — opportunities!

Right-brain person, meet left-brain person; left-brain, meet right. Get to know each other — because of your differences, when you get to know each other and understand those differences, you'll open up a whole new way of looking at challenges.

The whole "right-brain is this type of person, left-brain is that type" is, of course, somewhat of a convenient simplification.

But it's a simplification based on a more sophisticated system of brain and behavior types initially developed from the original split-brain research of Nobel Prize-winning Roger Sperry, PhD, professor at California Institute of Technology.

Sperry studied a number of people with severe epilepsy whose brains had been bisected through the corpus callosum, which connects the two hemispheres of the brain together. When the connection was severed, each person functioned with two separate minds. As a result, he was able to conduct tests to see how each hemisphere processed information without interference from the other hemisphere.

The results of Sperry's study of left-brain/right-brain traits, overlaid with Dr. Paul MacLean's hypothesis of the triune brain, produced numerous breakthroughs in our understanding of how our brains work. (Dr. MacLean was a leading scientist at the National Institute of Mental Health.)

The triune brain hypothesis argues that there are three separate evolutionary levels to our brains:

- The reptilian, our innermost layer, the residence of the fight-or-flight instinct and the most primitive layer. Territorial and selfish.
- The limbic system, the middle layer where emotions reside, as well as our memory systems. Social and nurturing.
- The neocortex, the outer layer dealing with higher functions and language; this is what we call the executive brain, where decisions are made. Planning and abstract thinking.

Among these breakthroughs has been a continually deepening understanding of our brain and behavior preferences and orientations.

I call those different types of brain behavior *brainstyles*, and as a result of my research into the topic, I am working on a new book — *Brainstyles of the Rich and Famous: Thinking and Behavioral Patterns of Successful People* — about how our brainstyles affect our work, lifestyles, and success.

By "brainstyles" I mean our tendencies and preferences that are tied directly to the way our brains are wired and modified by our individual experiences. Wouldn't you love to know where your direct reports are coming from with their thinking? What I'm about to show you here is, in my opinion, the best way to do that, short of actual mind-reading.

## FEEDBACK LOG: PETER

Recently, I was conducting interviews for my next book, *Brainstyles of the Rich and Famous: Thinking and Behavioral Patterns of Successful People*. The subjects included many of the wealthiest, most talented, and greatest leaders in the country. They had all completed the Emergenetics Profile (which you'll soon encounter in this book), so I knew their thinking styles and behavior patterns before the interviews began.

My first interview was with the CEO and co-owner of one of the biggest franchise-based corporations in the world.

He scored high in the conceptual (big picture) and social (empathetic) thinking style and in the gregarious, driving, and yet flexible behavior patterns. Because I knew his test results before I interviewed him, I knew I needed only a small number of open-ended questions, and he just opened up. One story led to another, and he took me to various parts of the executive floor to introduce me to his leadership team. It was like an interview party. Nothing was linear or structured, and I just went with the flow.

The second interview was with one of *Forbes'* 100 Wealthiest People in the U.S., among the royalty of the business world. His profile was different from my first interview. Unlike my first interview subject, he was left-brain oriented but also demonstrated a strong right-brain preference (very big picture thinker). His behaviors were at the opposite end of the spectrum from my first interview: He was control-oriented and quiet, preferring to work alone.

I approached this interview with at least 40 questions and in a more structured way than my interviews with the franchise CEO. His answers were straightforward and short, no extra information added. No flow. I worked intently to get his story, background, and philosophy. Yes, he had stories, but he wasn't effusive. The good news was that I had been prepared by the Emergenetics Profile for what transpired in both interviews.

The learning point for me was trying to understand the person and the context of giving and receiving feedback. I had the profile to help me, but even if I hadn't, the Emergenetics model itself would have given me a framework from which to think about anybody I'm interacting with.

—Peter

As someone working on a team, with colleagues or direct reports, you have the opportunity to rethink your team in the same way.

The content of the feedback is only part of the interaction. Some of your direct reports, by their nature, are not outspoken or gregarious; you have to work harder to make the session go well. The rewards for everyone and the organization are worth the effort.

# EMERGENETICS

Like many of us, I spent years unconsciously "typing" people I worked with or encountered, often without measuring them against any sense of myself and the "type" of person I am.

I didn't give it a lot of thought — just made snap judgments that helped me better understand whom I was working with.

And they *were* judgments — "That person is an anal-retentive detail-freak" and similar categorizations. I can recall plenty of occasions when I thought something like, *I know what type of person this guy is* — without ever wondering if he was making similar snap judgments of the type of guy I was. Both of us were judging; neither of us sought any real understanding of the other.

I failed to see that understanding a person's brainstyle (i.e., not just what he thinks but also how he thinks), as reflected in his or her approach to life and work, involves just that: *understanding*, not judgment.

My eyes were opened — and then some! — when I encountered a dynamically new approach to understanding people's brain and behavior traits and preferences: the **Emergenetics® Profile**.

What I learned from Emergenetics — and I've been licensed and working with the program for more than 20 years now — can vastly increase the effectiveness of the feedback you offer.

Emergenetics was developed by Dr. Geil Browning, PhD from the University of Nebraska, and her research partner, Dr. Wendell Williams, PhD in developmental psychology, and a specialist in psychometrics.

Based on their research in psychology and neuroscience, they developed the Emergenetics Profile. Today, Dr. Browning is founder and CEO of Emergenetics International, with offices in the United States, Europe, and Asia. The Emergenetics Profile has given more than 400,000 businesspeople and educators worldwide a better understanding of why they think and behave as they do.

The intent is to help you better understand, first, yourself and, second, how each of your people performs and behaves, based on a four-quadrant brain model and three behavioral attributes.

You can already see how, once you have that better understanding, you'll be better prepared to provide — and receive — effective feedback.

I have used the Emergenetics Profile with executive leadership groups and employees from companies such as IBM, Apple, HP, Sun Life Financial, ReMax International, the DC Court System, and the U.S. Navy. Let me show you, briefly, how the profile works.

## COMPASS OF CONSCIOUSNESS

Emergenetics refers to "patterns of thinking and behaving that emerge from your genetic blueprint." Our thinking styles and behaviors stem from a combination of how our brains are wired and what we're exposed to through our environment and

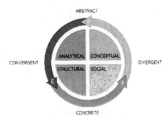

life experiences. In other words, nature and nurture come into play. The Emergenetics model takes into consideration both the genetic and the environmental factors, metaphorically dividing the brain into four major thinking attributes:

- Analytical
- Structural
- Social
- Conceptual

The above four traits or styles fall into the "how you think" arena. In addition, there are three basic spectrums within the "how you behave" category.

Now take a look at the following profile to get a clear view of what I'm talking about. This diagram reflects my own results, my personal Emergenetics Profile.

The circle is divided into four pie wedges. For me, the conceptual and social wedges are the largest, indicating that given the way my brain is wired and the way I've evolved through my life experiences, I'm mostly a Conceptual, Social thinker. That means I like seeing the big pic-

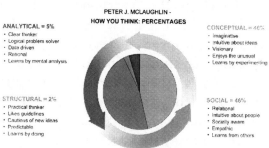

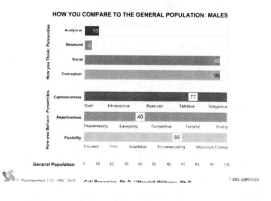

ture and am intuitive about ideas. (I appreciate details; they're just not my strength.) I like to interact with people and share ideas, but when it comes to details or a follow-up plan, my brain tends to leave the room. These are considered right-brain preferences. Knowing this about myself has been helpful in many situations.

For example, when it was time to hire a Director of Operations, I knew I needed to "team up" with someone who had more left-brain tendencies, to balance things out at the office — a "thinks things through and gets things done" kind of person. So I hired someone with left-brain tendencies (balanced with good social skills, because she had to deal with me!).

Take a look at her diagram:

You'll see that she prefers working from the Analytical and Structural areas. She's a practical, logical, and clear thinker, fantastic with details, and her social awareness, though not dominant in her profile, shows that she's interested in people — and could put up with my last-minute changes and ideas on projects. We complement each other well.

Of course, no one is 100% Analytical, or 100% Conceptual, or 100% anything. We are

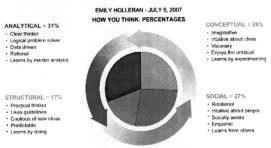

# EMERGENETICS® | PROFILE

EMILY HOLLERAN - JULY 5, 2007
HOW YOU THINK: PERCENTAGES

ANALYTICAL = 31%
· Clear thinker
· Logical problem solver
· Data driven
· Rational
· Learns by mental analysis

CONCEPTUAL = 26%
· Imaginative
· Intuitive about ideas
· Visionary
· Enjoys the unusual
· Learns by experimenting

STRUCTURAL = 17%
· Practical thinker
· Likes guidelines
· Cautious of new ideas
· Predictable
· Learns by doing

SOCIAL = 27%
· Relational
· Intuitive about people
· Socially aware
· Empathic
· Learns from others

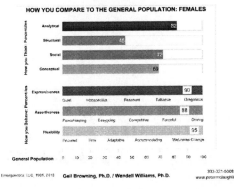

HOW YOU COMPARE TO THE GENERAL POPULATION: FEMALES

© Emergenetics LLC, 1991, 2012    Geil Browning, Ph.D. / Wendell Williams, Ph.D.    303-321-0008
www.petermclaughlin.com

all a combination of these four thinking preferences. But typically two or three will dominate (a dominant trait shows up in the profile as 23% or higher). One person might be mostly Analytical and Social. Another might be mostly Conceptual and Analytical. A third could be primarily Social, Structural, and Analytical. You get the idea.

And I suspect you are already getting a sense of how these ideas can affect — and improve — your feedback.

One executive, familiar and comfortable with her Structural and Social brainstyle, put her Emergenetics Profile and the following note on her door, with an arrow-and-heart calendar:

# EMERGENETICS® | PROFILE

HOW YOU THINK: PERCENTAGES

ANALYTICAL = 17%
- Clear thinker
- Logical problem solver
- Data driven
- Rational
- Learns by mental analysis

CONCEPTUAL = 12%
- Imaginative
- Intuitive about ideas
- Visionary
- Enjoys the unusual
- Learns by experimenting

STRUCTURAL = 38%
- Practical thinker
- Likes guidelines
- Cautious of new ideas
- Predictable
- Learns by doing

SOCIAL = 32%
- Relational
- Intuitive about people
- Socially aware
- Empathic
- Learns from others

I love you...

... but, make an
Appointment

## FEEDBACK LOG: PETER

A participant came up to me at the end of a recent speech to the first-line managers at Siemens Healthcare (part of Germany's enormous Siemens Company) in Philadelphia. My speech had discussed the use of Emergenetics in providing effective feedback.

The manager asked if I had a few minutes for her to speak with me. We sat down and she began to tell an interesting story about her recent "management review." She said it went horribly; both she and her manager, a senior VP, got upset; her manager was frustrated and she herself was crying.

After going through Emergenetics, she thought that her low performance rating from their session came from her inability to understand what her manager wanted for her to do and how she wanted it done.

She was convinced that her manager was a Conceptual/Analytical thinker who was only moderately flexible and expressive in her behavioral style. The manager would give general goals and wanted them done yesterday. The person I was speaking with liked her manager but seemed unable to do anything right for her. She herself was a very structured left-brain person, liked specifics, and was outgoing and social.

You see the problem/opportunity.

I told her that I had taken all the Siemens managers and leadership group through the Emergenetics workshop (including her manager), and I thought she should ask her manager for another meeting and a chance to discuss her review from the Emergenetics model point of view.

Some weeks later, I received an email explaining that the meeting had taken place with some good discussion (and even some laughter when they compared their profiles). Her manager set up a new review for a month later, during which time they would try to work out their communication and goal setting.

I find that the great thing about the Emergenetics Profile is that it's like a neutral fact finder. The profile just presents the facts (gleaned from your answers to the questions) and lets both parties see each other in new ways and then begin to work things out, with a lot less drama...even some fun.

As an Executive VP from IBM Global Services once said to me, "After I understood my profile and then saw others' profiles, it all made sense." She added: "What used to piss me off now makes me laugh."

Peter

# INTERLUDE

## TED TURNER AND TIGER WOODS – BRAINS AND BEHAVIORS

I met Ted Turner at Denver University's Daniels College of Business, where he was presenting some of his global ideas and giving feedback to comments and questions about his view of the world and his method of doing outrageous things, many of which helped change our way of life and improve the planet, as well as making him a multibillionaire. And some of which reduced his billions down to $1 billion (still not bad).

*Ted Turner*

In the Emergenetics parlance, he would be considered a right-brain preference guy. Big picture, conceptual, intuitive about ideas...Ted Turner didn't use focus groups; he "knew" what was missing and supplied it passionately...and for big bucks.

A perfect example of his intuitive thinking was his founding of CNN, which exactly nobody thought would work.

The idea for CNN germinated out of something that "pissed him off."

"I would get home from work [he was CEO at Turner Broadcasting] at 7 PM, and news would be over...and there wasn't another one until 11. So I never got to see the news. Availability 24/7 had a lot of appeal. I figured you couldn't do it with pure advertising; you'd need to have a subscriber fee."

Every major network had thought about a 24/7 news channel and all rejected the idea. Having done their left-brain research and focus groups, they thought it would be too expensive and nobody wanted news badly enough to pay a fee for it.

His feedback to them was: "Watch me!"

Though media was where he made his big money, his conceptual brain wandered far afield. He is the second-largest land owner in the country and a conservationist. On his land in Montana, "where the buffalo roamed," he had another untested idea: buffalo meat.

Turner had discovered the health aspects of bison meat and decided to open restaurants that specialize in serving up buffalo...*TED'S MONTANA GRILL*. It's doing quite well. Ted, the consummate salesman, told the D.U. crowd where his two restaurants were located in Denver to "please go eat there after my presentation."

If Ted Turner had worked for you, how would you change the way you gave feedback to him as opposed to, say, Tiger Woods — whom, though I've never met him, I have "scouted" (like a coach, which I used to be) and would place in the more left-brain preference camp.

Analytical in his thinking even down to how he constructs his practice sessions, Tiger seems to work well with coaches who approach golf with a more scientific and "bio-mechanics" approach to the game, like swing coach Sean Foley.

Ever watch Tiger putt? Pay attention to his "putting ritual," which never varies.

*Tiger Woods*

He walks to the opposite side of the hole, crouches and looks back at his ball; walks back behind his ball, crouches and looks again. Then he gets into his putting stance, but not quite up to the ball, and takes precisely two practice strokes. He then steps up to the ball, slightly widens his stance, looks at the hole, down to the ball; back to the hole, back down to the ball...then putts.

Every time, all the time.

When Tiger gives feedback to the announcers after his round, he analyzes his shots with a calm, almost detached observation. Players remark about his ability to "manage the course," though not always his reactions, especially to a bad shot.

As with J. K. Rowling (Harry Potter author), whom we will discuss in Chapter Six, Tiger's behavioral profile would be more in the "controlled, less expressive" range. Totally unlike Ted Turner, who lives life out loud.

If Tiger and Ted were both on your leadership team, I would coach you to listen well, have your facts straight, and be flexible.

# EMERGENETICS MEETS FEEDBACK

Here's how I make use of this information come feedback time.

Say I've got 10 direct reports. I try to analyze each one based on what I observe, using the Emergenetics model for thinking and behavioral styles. I might come to the conclusion that this one is a clear thinker, and that one is inventive and less practical. Of course instead of just guessing, I actually get my direct reports to take the survey so I have their profiles in hand.

I find that one of my people loves numbers, likes clarity, likes structure. When I do feedback with this person, I'll definitely give her a specific agenda, a time we're going to start our meeting, and a time we're going to finish. She will probably want to sit at a desk or in an office around a table, and she'll want some written feedback. Her day is structured and scheduled, so I have to make sure to keep an eye on the clock and not go over the time we've allotted for our feedback session.

I see that another of my direct reports is very much a right-brained person. He's going to want feedback eyeball to eyeball. He'll want it to be straightforward, but at the same time, he wouldn't mind if I presented it in an unconventional, fun way. He'll want the big picture before we get into any details. In consideration of his nature, I give him space to think and develop his creative ideas.

Next I've got someone who loves people. If possible, I use less email with him — this is someone I know I want to talk to person-to-person or on the phone. I need to set up a friendly atmosphere when giving him feedback. The agenda is not as important to someone whose predominant trait is social. I do need to pay special attention to my people skills, though, making sure to listen carefully and make good eye contact. Building a relationship is a lot more important to this person than facts and figures will ever be (though you need both, of course).

By knowing the individual thinking preferences of everyone on my team, I can deliver feedback that'll be more relevant and appealing to each person. My job is to couch my feedback message based on the way I perceive their thinking preferences. In the end, this benefits them, me, and our entire company. If I'm delivering feedback in a totally inappropriate style for the person sitting in front of me, I lose, he or she loses, and we both go down. Don't let this happen. Take the time to understand each person's thinking preferences well before your feedback session.

And when you do, be aware that there's more to how our minds work than how our brains work.

## BEHAVE YOURSELF

People like to believe that they control how they live their lives by how the brain processes the world. But in reality the course of their lives is often mitigated by behaviors, traits, learned and acquired preferences — the full spectrum of factors that shape our lives that make us human.

One of the things I find most effective about Emergenetics is its inclusion of behavioral traits (separated from brain preferences) among the factors analyzed in the profile.

For each of these behavioral attributes, there's a range or a continuum of possibilities, as you'll see in the following diagrams:

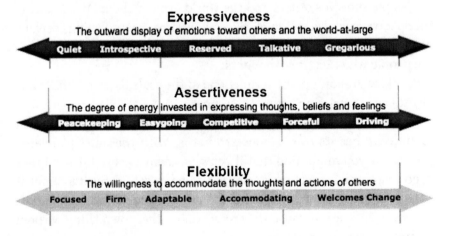

As with thinking preferences, there's no right or wrong here. There are simply behavioral preferences that each of us possesses, which are modified as we interact with our environment. Sometimes others can decipher our thinking preferences by the way we behave, but not often.

Our behavior can diverge radically from what we're actually thinking, making it harder for people to read us.

When you look at your direct report, and he behaves a certain way, realize that this behavior may or may not be consistent with his thinking preferences.

Some people are far more expressive than others; there may be great depth to their thinking in either case.

If you as a manager come on too strong during a feedback session with a person at the "reserved" end of the scale, don't be surprised if he backs off and retreats into the comfort zone of his own thoughts. You have to know the emotional makeup as well as the thinking preferences of the person you're giving feedback to. Behavior is closely tied to emotional makeup. Let's take a moment to explore each behavioral attribute individually.

**Expressiveness**
The outward display of emotions toward others and the world-at-large

| Quiet | Introspective | Reserved | Talkative | Gregarious |
|-------|---------------|----------|-----------|------------|

**Expressiveness:** This attribute indicates the amount of social interest people show for others and the world around them. At one end of the spectrum you've got quiet, likes alone time, keeps feelings private. At the other end you've got spontaneous, gregarious, performer. These are people who talk their thoughts.

People who show up on the quiet end of the scale listen carefully and digest the information before they speak.

Where do your direct reports fall within this spectrum? Realize that each group has its own unique strengths. With the quiet people on your team, you might find that if you give them a project, they'll take it, go away with it, work on it solo, and come back to deliver it completed to your satisfaction. But during the process you don't have a handle on where they are because they're off doing their own thing without communicating back to you.

**Assertiveness**
The degree of energy invested in expressing thoughts, beliefs and feelings

| Peacekeeping | Easygoing | Competitive | Forceful | Driving |
|--------------|-----------|-------------|----------|---------|

**Assertiveness:** This attribute reflects the degree of energy invested in expressing thoughts, beliefs, and feelings. At one end of the continuum are people who are peacekeeping and easygoing. They believe that winning isn't everything and would rather be the peacemakers of the group. At the other end, you've got forceful and driving. These are people who prefer to lead, are competitive in most situations, and embrace confrontation.

Everyone has a comfortable range of assertiveness, and everyone is capable of moving to other points along the spectrum as needed in just about any situation. Temporary adjustments can be made, and sometimes need to be made. For example, we need drivers on our teams, but we also need them to recognize that certain people are assertive and that sometimes they have to hold back a little. (The further you go out of your comfort zone, the more anxious you become. If a peacemaker plays the role of hard-driving leader for too long, he'll be stressed and exhausted.)

So as a team leader, I have every right (as well as a responsibility) to walk up to my direct report and say, "Harry, every meeting we're in, you dominate the meeting. We've got to use some restraint. Yes, we want you to be a driver. We need decision-makers like you. But we also want you to understand that you need to be conscious of this particular strength, because it can dominate a meeting and take away everyone else's chance. For you to become a great leader, you've got to learn to alter your assertiveness in certain situations."

**Flexibility**

The willingness to accommodate the thoughts and actions of others

Focused     Firm     Adaptable     Accommodating     Welcomes Change

**Flexibility:** This behavioral attribute measures the willingness to accommodate the thoughts and actions of others. People who are more flexible are better able to handle ambiguous situations without losing their temper. In this portion of the spectrum you'll find open-mindedness, patience around difficult people, and a desire to elevate other people's self-esteem. These individuals are equipped to meet others more than halfway, with the goal of achieving a win-win situation. This skill represents the "chaos is cool" crowd, those who are comfortable with cultural changes. The people at the other end of the scale might be seen as being more focused, having stronger opinions, and disliking change. You can look to them, however, to be keepers of the culture, sometimes to the extreme.

The flexibility spectrum also shows how comfortable or uncomfortable a person feels in different situations. Use this knowledge to benefit the recipient of the feedback.

Some people like well-defined situations. When I give feedback to these individuals, I bring them to my office or some other formal setting where I know they'll be comfortable. Maybe we'd even meet in *their* office where they really feel at ease.

With more flexible individuals, it doesn't matter as much. I can give them feedback in the hallway, or walking around campus, or over a cup of coffee at a nearby café. They're flexible about it.

The point is, by understanding both the thinking and behavior preferences of your direct reports, you can dynamically increase the effectiveness of your feedback as well as the level of enthusiasm your direct reports bring to the Feedback Culture you are creating.

## BE PREPARED TO BE SURPRISED

Here's a story that puts all the elements of thinking and behavior traits into place — and serves as a good reminder that not everything is obvious at first glance.

I know an engineer who some time ago worked as an intern for a medical electronics engineering firm while she was still in college studying engineering. Let's call her Sue.

Sue was given an assignment, and for the next two months she pretty much went off and did her own thing. She was polite and reserved, always had a smile for everyone, chatted occasionally with a fellow intern and the department's administrative assistant, spoke with her immediate supervisor when necessary, but otherwise hardly interacted with anyone.

Sue's supervisor gave her the freedom to come and go at will, since her assignment involved doing a lot of research at a nearby technical library. He met with her once a week to see how she was progressing; other than that, she had free rein. Meanwhile, the department head neither understood nor liked any of this. This intern never attended meetings, hardly talked with senior engineers, and came and went as she pleased. This girl, he thought, is taking us for a ride.

But when at the end of her two months there she gave a polished, high-level presentation to the division, outlining in great technical detail her findings and recommendations, the department head was floored.

Because Sue was reserved around him, he had no idea she was legitimate, until she proved her worth at that presentation.

So the lesson here is this: Don't underestimate your reserved people. They may end up being some of your best performers.

It's a lesson that, with obvious adjustments for particular behaviors, should be applied to *all* of your people, not just the ones who seem at first glance to be reserved.

The better you know your direct reports, and the more open you remain to letting them surprise you, the more effective and influential your feedback will be.

## BARTERING WITH FEEDBACK

Now let's revisit Sue, that reserved employee who aced the presentation, surprising her manager and everyone else.

She "did her own thing, her own way" and it worked out well for all concerned. But it could just as easily have gone the other way. The presentation could have been a disaster.

Time for feedback!

The fact that the ultimate outcome was positive is certainly something that should be stressed when providing post-presentation feedback to the employee. In fact, you can probably build a small catalog of positive feedback elements out of her presentation performance. Keep them in mind — you'll need them.

The positive outcome of the presentation is not the most important point here. The most important point is that the employee must come to understand that while her ultimate performance was stellar, her "go her own way" approach up to the moment she took the stage is unacceptable.

*Managers must have communications from their direct reports, no matter how much the direct report dislikes the process* — that is why they're called *reports.*

The feedback challenge in this situation is to arrive at a bartered agreement with the employee whereby she agrees to report on a frequent and consistent basis, and you agree to adjust — only so much as you are comfortable — matters so that she can work "her way" as much as possible.

Win-win.

You help develop an employee who has large potential, and she begins to overcome a deficit that could affect her in her current position and might prevent her from rising in the organization.

This is a terrific example of how effective, carefully designed and presented feedback works on multiple levels. You have just:

- Reinforced her positive qualities
- Addressed an employee's performance and your expectations for necessary changes in some details of her performance
- Negotiated an acceptable and comfortable shift in her behavior while acknowledging your understanding of the strengths of her brain and behavioral styles

The benefits of this level of feedback will flow to the company and to the employee — and that's how feedback achieves win-win-win.

## TIPS, TOOLS, & TACTICS

**TIP:** The nature of our individual brainstyles and behaviors can affect the way we respond to feedback.

**TIP:** Take time to understand the brainstyles and behaviors of those you work with and adjust your language and communication style to suit theirs.

**TIP:** Pay attention to how new team members — and long-term ones too — respond to various situations and contexts. Their reactions and how they express them will help you better understand their thinking and behavior styles.

TOOL: Use the Emergenetics model as a "scouting report." Write notes in the applicable boxes to help you better understand your colleagues or direct reports.

TOOL: The Emergenetics Profile, taken on the Web, can provide more, exact, and useful insights into the nature of your direct reports. They will love knowing more about themselves and you, and they can form better, more efficient and productive teams.

| EMERGENETICS™ TEMPLATE | |
|---|---|
| Analytical | Conceptual |
| Structural | Social |
| Expressiveness<br>Assertiveness<br>Flexibility | |

**TOOL:** Make yourself a small pocket reminder of your preferences, of where your thinking style places you on the Emergenetics circle. This little symbolic reminder of those qualities most prominent in your makeup, and those less prominent, can give you "cues" at a glance, prompting you to make extra effort to ensure that your feedback represents all the qualities of thought, not just those that are well-developed.

**TACTIC:** A feedback session, properly prepared for and executed, is an excellent opportunity to barter with employees, enhancing their effectiveness with the structure you require while providing them with additional "freedoms" that reflect their particular work- and brainstyles.

**TACTIC:** Review the details that support the content of your feedback, and make sure that you include only those details absolutely necessary to make your immediate points. Don't risk overwhelming — or losing — your message in a mass of extraneous detail.

**TACTIC:** Discuss Emergenetics with your team members, and ask if they would be interested in taking the program as a group (resources and budget permitting, of course).

At the back of this book, you'll find more information about Emergenetics, including links to its Web site. Take a look — I can guarantee you'll find Emergenetics fascinating.

*If I were given the opportunity
to present a gift to the next generation,
it would be the ability for each individual
to learn to laugh at himself."*

Charles M. Schulz, cartoonist

*I'll have someone from my generation get in touch*

*with someone from your generation.*

## CHAPTER FIVE

## FEEDBACK ACROSS THE GENERATIONS

Do you find as much grievance as guffaw in the cartoon at the head of this chapter? You're not alone.

Differences among the generations are nothing new, of course. They weren't new in the 1960s, when the term "Generation Gap" became common. They weren't new, for that matter, in Shakespeare's time, or even earlier.

Prowl among the artifacts of the earliest civilizations, the bits and scraps of writing that have survived from the dawn of civilization, and you'll come across ancient wisdom along the lines of: *Things aren't what they used to be. The new generation doesn't—*

You get the picture.

Differences among the generations, and the communications challenges those differences pose, are as old as our species.

What is new about the times we live in is the *number of generations working side-by-side.*

While at one time it was common for multi-generational families to work a farm, or for one generation to follow another into the same factory, what's happened over the past few decades is different.

People are living longer and working longer. As a result, it's not unusual to find four generations in one work environment today.

The opportunities and benefits of this situation are huge — yet they are opportunities and benefits that are rarely harvested, and often ignored entirely, because of that age-old "generation gap" and the communications complications it carries.

The real problem is a *communication* gap, not solely a generational gap.

Either way, it's still a gap, and one that any number of good ideas, innovations, improvements, and insights fall into and are never heard from again.

What to do about it?

Put in place a new approach to feedback — a feedback revolution! — that acknowledges, adjusts for, and above all celebrates the resources and perspectives that different generations bring to the workplace.

## WHOSE GENERATION GAP?
## SHAKESPEARE REVISITED

I'll bet that by the time you finish this chapter — and maybe even before — you'll see that effective feedback, by its very nature, works with every generation. You just have to tailor its presentation and delivery to match the recipient.

But, as the previous chapters showed, you would be doing that anyway, whether the recipient is 20 years older than you, 20 years younger, or born on the same date in the same year as you.

At the same time, there are some *general* generational differences to keep in mind; understanding these differences and using that understanding to guide your feedback will go a long way toward ensuring that your message isn't swallowed by the generation gap.

And there's one specific difference in today's workplace, a difference that makes it vital for managers to develop their cross-generational understanding. The difference? Simple:

*For the first time, it's becoming common to have four and, in some cases, five generations represented among the workers in a single company.*

This is new, and it's a situation that presents enormous opportunities as well as challenges.

Two and often three generations working a family farm was once the norm, of course. Likewise, many industries saw several generations of workers pass through its gates, the younger apprenticed to the older, following in their parents' footsteps. It's the stuff of our history, and of a surprising number of novels and movies.

Right there is a *big* difference between the old days and the present, between *then* and *now*.

In an era where many if not most occupations, including professions as well as skilled labor, involved an apprenticeship, generations working alongside each other was common — and, critically, *structured*. The younger worker was apprenticed to an older one for a period of time during which the experience, knowledge, and skill involved in the job was passed from the senior generation to the junior.

Things are different today. While many businesses and organizations do institute mentoring programs for younger team members, that process differs in many ways from the cross-generational training that apprenticeship provided.

Did you ever wonder where the word "mentor" and the concept it represents came from?

I went to a Jesuit school where they still taught the classics, many in the original Latin or Greek. My favorite was the *Odyssey*, Homer's great adventure of "the wily Odysseus" traveling home from the tragic war fought over Helen of Troy.

Odysseus had the foresight before he left for the battle to request the services of his old friend Mentor to help his wife, Penelope, take care of their only son, Telemachus, while Odysseus was gone. As it turned out, he was

> gone for 20 long years, during which time Mentor acted as an advisor and teacher to the young Telemachus. (I hope he had an overtime clause in his contract.)
>
> He did such a good job that his name is remembered to this day as one who listens, advises, and guides. His name, though few know his story, is spread throughout the halls of business and sports. In times of great change and many generations working together, mentorship is a key ingredient for surviving and perhaps even thriving in the new environment.

More critically, in terms of feedback, many young workers are thrown directly into the workforce at higher than entry-level positions. For the "best and the brightest," the "Whiz Kids," or whatever the cream of each year's crop from our most prestigious universities and advanced degree programs is called, those positions — and salaries — can be *far* higher than traditional entry-level posts.

Today's multi-generational workforce is not a consequence of family ownership (although that obviously still applies in certain cases); nor is it a product of proximity to the local factory.

Rather, the spread of ages in a company today is the result of factors that have been building for the last half-century:

- People are living longer, and are thus working longer — whether by choice or necessity.
- More than that, people are remaining vigorously engaged with their work longer.
- At the same time, the youngest generations entering the workplace are doing so with skills — and outlooks — shaped not only by previous generations including their parents, but also by an educational, social, and technological landscape that is in many ways radically different from what preceded it.

Additionally, as a result of the technological upheavals of the last couple of decades, the organizational structure and particularly the relationship among the generations within that structure have been altered.

> If you've ever accompanied a child to college, you've had a great first-hand glimpse of generational differences: the dorm room!
>
> No matter what generation you're from, the next generation's dorm rooms tend to strike you as:
> - Wilder
> - More comfortable
> - More technologically sophisticated
> - Less clean

The "Whiz Kid Effect" — think Bill Gates and Steve Jobs a quarter-century ago, Mark Zuckerberg more recently, and dozens of others of varying levels of spectacular success or failure in between — has seen some very young people running or managing very large companies, including some much older employees.

This, too, is different. While long shelves of novels and movies offer windows into how previous eras handled the cross-generational challenge, that handling generally fell into a fairly narrow range:
- "Old Bull" Versus "Young Bull"
- Wise Elder Teaches Young Whippersnapper a Lesson or Two
- Young Whippersnapper Teaches Wise Elder a Lesson or Two
- Elder and Whippersnapper Never Do Learn Anything and Destroy the Company in the Process

There are variations, of course — Young Whippersnapper Marries Wise Elder's Child (which was Wise Elder's plan all along) — but those are the basics.

What they have in common was that for all the drama — or comedy — in the telling, they reaffirmed a "natural order of things": young people growing into the roles formerly held by their elders. In other words:

*To everything, there is a season...*

Another famous approach to the passing of time can be found in Shakespeare's *As You Like It*, which has reminded us since 1600 that as we move through the ages of life, we also move through different roles — from youthful exuberance (and joyful foolhardiness!) to elderly wisdom (and infirmity). You remember the passage — but in case you don't (and even if you do!), I've included it in a sidebar. The passage is as poignant and accurate today as it was more than four centuries ago.

### As the Bard Said...

All the world's a stage,
And all the men and women merely players:
They have their exits and their entrances;
And one man in his time plays many parts,
His acts being seven ages. At first, the infant,
Mewling and puking in the nurse's arms.
And then the whining school-boy, with his satchel
And shining morning face, creeping like snail
Unwillingly to school. And then the lover,
Sighing like furnace, with a woeful ballad
Made to his mistress' eyebrow. Then a soldier,
Full of strange oaths and bearded like the pard,
Jealous in honour, sudden and quick in quarrel,
Seeking the bubble reputation
Even in the cannon's mouth. And then the justice,
In fair round belly with good capon lined,
With eyes severe and beard of formal cut,
Full of wise saws and modern instances;
And so he plays his part. The sixth age shifts
Into the lean and slipper'd pantaloon,
With spectacles on nose and pouch on side,
His youthful hose, well saved, a world too wide
For his shrunk shank; and his big manly voice,
Turning again toward childish treble, pipes
And whistles in his sound. Last scene of all,
That ends this strange eventful history,
Is second childishness and mere oblivion,
Sans teeth, sans eyes, sans taste, sans everything.

William Shakespeare,
*As You Like It*

Now, clearly you won't be working with the first or second of Shakespeare's Ages — if you have infant or child employees, you've got larger labor law challenges than feedback can resolve! — and likely not with the seventh. But all those "stages" in between may be represented in your workforce, perhaps even on a single team. Shakespeare's catalog has some useful reminders for dealing with each of them.

But these aren't Shakespeare's times.

These aren't even Neil Simon's times anymore!

It's no surprise to anyone whose eyes and ears are open that the "natural order" has been turned upside down, pulled inside out, and twisted sidewise by the societal changes mentioned above. *Every* generation is working next to every other generation now, and *that's* the *new* natural order of things.

In this multi-generational workforce, a manager must know how to reach each age group with effective feedback.

But as I've shown throughout this book, effective feedback has as much to do with your sense of the brainstyle of the person you're providing feedback to as it does with the content of the feedback itself.

Let's make that even more clear:

- Effective feedback seamlessly combines content — the feedback message — with your understanding of the brainstyle of the person receiving the feedback.
- The two are mutually reinforcing, and, ultimately, inextricable.

If we approach the modern, multi-generational workforce with these thoughts in mind, and broaden our definition of generations to create a sort of "generational brainstyle" that can be combined with our understanding of the specific brainstyles of specific employees where appropriate, well...

*You will be able to tailor your feedback both to the employee's particular needs and to that employee's generational expectations.*

Let's take a look at the four generations currently in our workforce, and I'll show you exactly what I mean.

# FEEDBACK LOG: MARGIE

A few months back I was playing a jazz gig at a local family-friendly restaurant. A family of three — Mom, Dad, and young son (I judged him to be about five) — were seated in a corner. I noticed that the young boy was pointing to me, talking to his mom, asking questions; they were having an animated exchange. On break, I went over to introduce myself and have a quick visit.

After telling me his name, Nathan looked at his mom and said, "Ask her." His mom said, "You ask her — she's right here."

Nathan surprised me by asking if I would sing "Route 66." How in the world would a five-year-old even know that old standard, much less request it?

I said that I would be delighted to.

After the song, I said to the audience that Nathan had requested it. He was proud to be mentioned from the stage and came up to put a dollar in the tip jar.

I asked him how he knew the song — and let him speak into the mic.

Nathan's reply: "The movie *Cars*, silly!"

The audience went crazy.

And I was reminded that different generations have different experiences of the same things, and have more in common than you might think.

But you have to ask to find out.

Margie

# YOU CAN'T JUDGE A GENERATION BY ITS NICKNAME

As the earlier chapters of this book demonstrated, your understanding of both the behavioral styles and the thinking styles of other people plays a large role in helping you tailor your feedback.

The situation is similar with the various generations, but, as with individual assessments, a template created to profile a generation is a *starting place*, not the final word.

Keep that in mind as we look at the four generations currently in the workplace.

# GENERATION Y: THE TWENTY-SOMETHINGS

The youngest members of the workforce, Generation Y, also known as Millennials, were born between the mid-1980s and the early 21st century. There are more than 70 million members of this generation, and they are making themselves known in the workforce — and in the arts, politics, and every other aspect of our culture. Facebook founder Mark Zuckerberg is a member of Generation Y, as is Justin Bieber.

Of course, there's always a new crop of twenty-somethings coming along. And each new generation of twenty-somethings tends to have a new nickname bestowed upon it. In the 1950s they were the Beats, the 1960s saw the hippies, and so on.

These generational labels try to categorize a generation that really doesn't like to be pigeonholed, which is at least mildly ironic. And it is probably true of all twenty-something populations throughout history: This is the age at which ambition and energy rise close to their highest levels, the hormone-driven enthusiasms of the adolescent both tempered and enhanced by a few more years of experience, education, and, frankly, impatience with the older generation of bosses, governments, and parents.

Those who are about 18 to 30 years old tend to be:

- **Selective** — They don't automatically accept "traditional values" handed down from previous generations. They pick what they feel is the best from previous generations and from worldwide influences.
- **Connected** — This generation values instant and constant connectedness above nearly everything else.
- **Eclectic** — Again, this stems from a greater global awareness.
- **Authentic** — They can't stand insincerity. Just tell it as it is.
- **Enterprising** — With the economy fluctuating, many have turned to starting their own side businesses built upon personal interests.
- **Flexible regarding gender roles** — This is the least racist/sexist generation we have ever seen; women can be engineers, astronauts, CEOs, doctors. Men can be nurses, fashion consultants, at-home dads. Race plays a minimal to nonexistent role in Generation Y thinking and decision-making. There really are no more limitations gender-wise, sex-preference-wise, or race-wise as this generation sees it.
- **Multi-taskers** — Thanks in part to the proliferation of personal electronic devices, they are confident that they can perform different tasks simultaneously; research is incomplete on the accuracy of this belief. They tend to have sharp minds and good reflexes.

Generation Y employees appreciate feedback that's honest and direct. They like to keep things moving; long meetings and sessions fail to keep their interest. You've got to get to the point quickly — forget the small talk. But it's perfectly acceptable to spend a few moments asking them how things are going, or talking about a mutually interesting topic, in a friendly, genuine manner. Because their time is valuable to them, Generation Y members don't want to waste it reading lengthy reports. Summaries and bulleted items are a must for any written feedback.

They love technology. Email, cell phones, text messaging, PowerPoint, laptops — it's all good. Facebook and Twitter and LinkedIn! Connectedness is more than a skill or convenience for Gen Y employees — it's a need that's also often perceived as a right.

Incorporate technology during your feedback session. How about opening your laptop and bringing up some colorful PowerPoint slides? (Just don't overdo it — as we'll see in the next chapter.)

One thing I especially like about the Generation Y twenty-something age group is that they love getting feedback. They don't want long-winded speeches. They don't need to be preached to. They do want to know where they stand, how they're performing, and what you think of their work. They want feedback, as well as encouragement, on a consistent basis. And typically they're not afraid of criticism. They want open dialogue, and they expect it to be a two-way street.

They like a challenge, and they hate to be bored. Typically well-educated, they enjoy learning new things, but they prefer getting their information in sound bites and highlights. Generation Y appreciates a friendly demeanor and a sense of humor.

As writer Ryan Healy has pointed out, his generation already knows that feedback is most effective when it flows both ways: "Give me feedback! And hear me out, too."

Your strategy when giving someone in his or her twenties feedback, then, is to be frank and straightforward. Keep the session friendly but brief. Make use of technology. Avoid long written reports; instead, stick to summaries and lists. Be sincere and, most of all, real. Relevancy is very important to this age group. So is spontaneity. Why not take a twenty-something to a coffee shop and offer feedback there?

In fact, why don't *I* offer some feedback right here? Let's look at some specific approaches to providing feedback to twenty-something employees:

# TIPS, TOOLS, & TACTICS: GENERATION Y

## TIPS
- Be specific, as with *all* feedback.
- Use twenty-somethings' impatience to your advantage — set up goals and deliverables that can be achieved quickly (set up incremental or staged goals if necessary).
- Conversely, use your feedback sessions to begin to show twenty-somethings that in some cases, slower and steadier wins better races.

## TOOLS

- Use Generation Y's technology comfort levels to your advantage — and to the advantage of your feedback! Email, text messages, video chats, and PowerPoint presentations can be effective feedback tools with twenty-somethings.
- Get to your point quickly, using only as much time as needed.

## TACTICS

- Make lists and summaries of feedback — and have the twenty-something employee do the same. Then compare lists!
- Don't forget to add humor — and, if appropriate, irony — to your feedback sessions.

# GENERATION X: THE LATCHKEY KIDS — JUNE CLEAVER HAS LEFT THE HOUSE

Born between the mid-1960s and the 1980s, the forty-somethings are generally classified as Generation Xers. Again, what comes to mind is the end of an era and the start of new thinking, new freedoms, new ways of viewing the world. This group has seen swift and dramatic changes in science, technology, medicine, television, politics, the economy, and pretty much everything else under the sun.

They are also a generation that was handed large responsibility — or the opportunity for it — early on. Another description applied to the generation was *Latchkey Kids* — a term that reflects the entry of this generation's mothers into the workforce in large numbers.

For many Gen X children, June Cleaver had left the house. The kids were responsible for letting themselves in after school, for entertaining themselves, for dealing with day-to-day problems and challenges as they arose. As a result, this is a very practical generation, accustomed to taking care of things themselves.

Not surprisingly, this age group likes to experience things firsthand. They like to be part of a community, to contribute, to make an impact, to be heard, to make a difference. They're not afraid to learn by trial and error.

Some adjectives that describe this group include:
- **Open-minded** — They are open to new ideas and innovations, and they're comfortable with diversity in the workplace.
- **Practical** — They like to get the job done efficiently and then move on to whatever's next.
- **Desire recognition** — When they do a good job, they know it, but they like being recognized for it.
- **Well-educated** — This group came of age during the Information Age and knows how to get around the Web.
- **Independent** — Freedom to complete a project their way without a lot of supervision is important to most forty-somethings.
- **Flexible** — They'll be flexible with you, and they'll expect you to be flexible as well.

Forty-somethings believe in possibilities.

They accept diversity.

They look at all sides of a situation, and they're not afraid to say, "I'm not sure" or "I don't know."

Generation X employees would rather remain uncertain for a period of time than jump to the wrong conclusion.

When you give feedback to someone in this age group, you've got to keep several things in mind. First, for this generation things aren't black and white. There are many in-between shades of gray, and many possible ways to approach a problem, and just as many possible solutions. You need to know that this is a practical group. They're certainly comfortable with technology, but mainly as a means to an end. They view the computer as a tool, a necessity, but they aren't gung-ho about the latest technological gizmos like members of Generation Y tend to be. They question rules, and they respect them only if, in their view, there's a good reason to have the rule in place.

Keeping all this in mind, here's how you can give a forty-something good feedback:

Maintain a friendly attitude and a casual demeanor.

Have an open mind during the session, and offer plenty of opportunities for back-and-forth dialogue. In other words, don't do all the talking — let the other person do some of the talking, questioning, and even evaluating. Generation Xers like to participate in their own evaluation.

You don't need to go overboard with technology. The person you're giving feedback to might expect a paper copy of his or her evaluation. Members of Generation X will look for direction from you, but at the same time they'll expect a large degree of freedom and flexibility to complete their tasks. When you make a request, always give your reason behind it, and always be prepared to listen to a rebuttal. Let them share their point of view with you.

Understand that many Gen Xers don't quite trust authority. You don't get respect automatically just because you're the boss. You have to earn respect through your character, integrity, honesty, and by treating others fairly. This generation isn't big on bureaucracy and corporate politics, so during your feedback session, skip any unnecessary paperwork and procedures. Keep it real, keep it relevant, and always show the other person respect.

And note that life balance is important to this age group. Many have young children at home. Perhaps remembering the downside of latchkey afternoons as well as its advantages, they won't think twice about saying no to overtime in order to spend more time with the kids. Definitely have expectations and express them, but don't expect a forty-something to stick around for long if your demands become unreasonable.

When you offer feedback, make sure you recognize the person's individual contributions. And do it in a timely manner. Generation X employees prefer getting feedback and recognition sooner rather than later. They also like learning new things, so this is a good group to send to training programs. Most of the time, they'll love it.

After you've given clear feedback and you've given the other person the chance to respond, let the person run with the project. Don't expect weekly written reports. Don't expect the forty-something to be satisfied with tedious, repetitive work. Do expect her or him to enjoy a good challenge. This age group likes getting the job done and moving on to the next activity.

To summarize, with Generation X, you shouldn't do all the talking during a feedback session.

# TIPS, TOOLS, & TACTICS: GENERATION X

## TIPS

- Generation X loves challenges: Make sure not only that their work includes challenging projects and responsibilities, but also that your feedback includes new challenges.
- Find areas where flexibility and nonstandard approaches to tasks and responsibilities can be introduced or implemented.
- Treat the other person with respect and allow him or her to be an active participant in the discussion.

## TOOLS

- Use technology to enhance and extend feedback sessions.
- Think about providing a printed copy of their evaluation, something tangible they can take home.
- Don't be shy about offering them further training if you feel — or, more importantly, if *they* feel (accurately, of course) — that their potential is not fully being tapped.

## TACTICS

- Limit feedback-related paperwork as much as possible.
- Get to the point quickly and clearly, focusing as much energy on the consequences and ongoing opportunities that result from the feedback as on the feedback itself.
- Bear in mind that Generation X employees are likely to be resistant to responsibilities that limit their time with family — negotiate the balance that best suits your employee's family concerns as well as your business goals.
- Offer direction balanced with plenty of freedom and flexibility for them to complete the project their way, incorporating their creativity and innovation.
- Reward good performance swiftly — don't wait.

# INTERLUDE

## GEN Y: TAYLOR SWIFT: SINGING YOUR FEEDBACK OUT LOUD

## GEN X/JONES: J. K. ROWLING: RESERVED...SPEAKING THROUGH HARRY POTTER

Taylor Swift, one of the phenoms of the music industry — has an interesting way of giving feedback to ex-boyfriends and creating hit songs at the same time. A recent hit, "We Are Never Ever Getting Back Together," was inspired by one of her ex-boyfriends...the exes list includes John Mayer and will soon add her most recent, Harry Styles. And her breakup song about Harry will add many coins (reportedly $47 million last year) to her purse.

*Taylor Swift*

Taylor Swift loves giving feedback. But will she love receiving it? According to a recent tweet, she say's, "No problem, bring it on."

She has recently tweeted that's it's fine if they want to write a song about her: "Fair's fair. If I'm gonna write songs about my exes, they can write about me. That's how it works" is what she said to *InStyle UK* magazine.

The digital natives of Generation Y grew up expressing their feelings out loud, or I should say "broadcasting" their thoughts and feelings and not being overly concerned as to who sees them.

"Tweeting" is an extension of their central nervous system..."I tweet, therefore I am."

Much of this Gen Y behavior is certainly more healthy than when I grew up in the "little children should be seen and not heard" generation. Being quiet and sitting still in straight-line rows won you a blue ribbon (only one, by the way) back then. Giving feedback to your teacher was not encouraged.

Singing your feedback to your direct reports (or to your boss for that matter) should not be attempted unless you are a very good singer, a decent songwriter, and the feedback contains very good news.

## HARRY POTTER GOES SUBVERSIVE

Someone who would never "go out loud" with her feelings, and works hard to maintain a private life, is J. K. Rowling. A *New Yorker* article by Ian Parker says, "She has a reputation for reserve: for being likable but shy and thin-skinned." Not at all like Gen Y's Taylor Swift, who says to her former boyfriends, "Bring it on."

J. K. Rowling was born in 1965, making her a late boomer/early Gen Xer, referred to by some as Generation Jones. Unlike Taylor Swift, who knew exactly what she wanted to do by her early teens and was aided and abetted by her parents, J. K. (or Jo, as her friends in Scotland call her) had an inkling she wanted to be a writer but was thwarted by her parents, who warned her that writing would never pay the bills.

Failure at almost everything she did, as she told a graduating class of Harvard students, ultimately set a

*J K Rowling*

ground floor for her to finish her first Harry Potter manuscript (while living at a poverty level that was just above homeless) out of desperation.

Like many Boomers, she was a rebel with new ideas about fantasy writing. "I was trying to subvert the genre," the way that most fantasies are built around clear ideas of good and evil. She built non-simplistic reality into her series; Harry and his friends grew and changed and tried to struggle with the complications of life.

Has she changed with her approximately $1 billion take from the Harry Potter series? The answer seems to be a resounding no.

Her feedback to those who say she should move from Great Britain to save millions of dollars on her taxes is this: She says she loves her country. Her "socialistic" country was there with a safety net when she went through hard times.

"I choose to remain a domiciled taxpayer for a couple of reasons...I wanted my children to grow up where I grew up...not free-floating expats, living in the limbo of some tax haven and associating only with children of similarly greedy tax exiles.

"A second reason, however, is that I'm indebted to the British welfare state...When my life hit rock bottom, that safety net...was there to break the fall...This, if you like, is my notion of patriotism."

Still a loyal, idealistic boomer after all these years.

## GENERATION JONES: LATE BOOMERS — MY MONEY OR MY LIFE

Born between the mid-1950s and the mid-1960s, a portion of the fifty-something crowd (formerly included with the boomers) is split between the Baby Boomers and Generation X. Some have dubbed this group Generation Jones, a separate category that came into existence in response to the realization that many within this group don't feel quite connected to the boomers or the Xers. According to the U.S. Department of Commerce Census Bureau, Generation Jones is the largest adult generation in the United States, accounting for more than a quarter of the country's population. Garth Brooks is a member of Generation Jones — and so is Barack Obama and more than 70 million other Americans.

So what characterizes the folks who belong to this large, influential group known as Generation Jones? "Responsibility" certainly comes to mind. This group juggles career with caring for growing kids and aging parents. No wonder so many fifty-somethings go through midlife crises!

Seriously, those who are in the Generation Jones age group have a lot on their minds — and did even before the economic upheavals of the last few years added to their worries, concerns, and plans.

Because they're juggling multiple responsibilities, and because they've already worked their way up the ladder, they tend to be discerning. On the job they may not hesitate to say no to one project and request a different assignment that fits better into their availability, philosophy, lifestyle, or interest level.

Some members of Generation Jones find themselves in the midst of a career transition. Maybe they're thinking about transferring to a different department. Or they're in the process of leaving behind what they've done for 25 years and starting something altogether new, like consulting work or a different career. A computer programmer might decide to go into marketing. An accountant might decide to start teaching a course at the local community college. This age group isn't keen on waiting for retirement to live their dreams. They want their jobs to be meaningful and satisfying.

You've got two basic camps of thinking within the Generation Jones group. There are those who are analyzing their present and long-term goals and positioning themselves to reach their dreams in the not-too-distant future. Life is short, time is running out, and dreams are important. It's now or never! This bunch tends to be more into risk-taking and into doing stuff like taking a sabbatical, seeing the world, or going on a spiritual retreat.

The second train of forty-something thought follows the money. Generation Jones looks at the mortgage they're still paying off, the cost of sending their kids to college in a few short years, and future nursing home and medical expenses they might have to help their parents with, and they decide they want a high-paying job. They're eyeing promotions and big bucks, and they prefer security over risk any day.

Within the fifty-something generation that harbors such widely varying ambitions, you'll find some common attributes. Adjectives to describe Generation Jones include:

- **Experienced** — Whether they've been at this company their entire career, or they've hopped around from one firm to another, or they're returning to work after having raised a family, these folks have accumulated an impressive collection of life and work experience.

- **Motivated** — With the "life is short" notion, they're motivated to succeed in some capacity (on the job, at home, through an outside interest) to find meaning and purpose.
- **Discerning** — They grew up with lots of choices available to them, and they like to be able to pick and choose.
- **High Earning Power** — Many are at the peak of their game salary-wise.
- **Searching** — They've stepped out of the "rat race" and are looking at the bigger picture of their lives.
- **Embrace Duality** — They are idealistic and cynical at the same time.
- **Mobile** — Unlike older generations, they're not particularly loyal to one company or brand, and they're comfortable moving from one place to another in search of a better job or a better community.

A fifty-something is a good "comparison shopper." If I don't like this group, I can transfer to that one over there. If my phone company's not giving me the best deal, I'll switch to another one. These folks want a good deal and high quality, and they usually find a way to have it both ways.

Giving feedback to this generation isn't that hard, but it helps to know where your fifty-something stands before you start. She's definitely motivated, but what motivates her? He's got a ton of experience in this particular area, but does he want to continue in the same arena or move on to something else? Will the promise of more money motivate your direct report to perform better, or is he looking for something different, such as more free time, longer vacations, or the opportunity to give back to society? Do your homework before sitting down and offering feedback. And don't be afraid to ask a few big questions, like:

- Are you where you want to be?
- Are you enjoying your job?
- How can I help you meet your home responsibilities so that you can perform better here?

Once you've asked questions like these, be open-minded to unconventional solutions. Seriously consider your Generation Jones employee's request to job share with a colleague, or to get a three-day weekend every other week in exchange for a pay adjustment. Consider telecommuting as a viable option. Learn to look at the world through his or her eyes. There's much more to life for many fifty-somethings than going to work and making money. Of course, for other fifty-somethings, work is everything! That's why "one size fits all" doesn't apply to this demographic group.

In general, when you offer feedback to someone in this group, don't go overboard with new technology. Even the Generation Jones members who are techno-geeks aren't always receptive to the latest, greatest gadgets that their younger counterparts readily embrace. Keep things fairly straightforward. Deliver feedback in a friendly, casual way. Point out areas that need improvement, but make sure you identify strengths and be generous with your praise.

To summarize, come up with different types of incentives for your fifty-somethings. Money and promotions will work for some. Others will be more motivated to perform well if you offer them other types of bonuses: a flexible schedule, more vacation time, a weekend retreat to a nice resort. Quality of life is important for this group. Try to be sensitive to a fifty-something's home responsibilities with family, including teenagers and older parents. This group has a lot on its mind — so find out what they're thinking and think outside the box to come up with mutually beneficial solutions.

# TIPS, TOOLS, & TACTICS: GENERATION JONES

## TIPS

- Generation Jones employees have reached the stage of their careers where they are willing — and determined — to be discerning. Be prepared for pushback or negotiation when offering new responsibilities or increased workload.
- Idealism and cynicism coexist in Generation Jones — address this duality in your feedback.
- Generation Jones is accustomed to having plenty of choices and options — structure your feedback sessions, if possible, in such a way as to offer choices, options, menus of possibilities.

## TOOLS

- Incentives are important to this generation — tailor your feedback to include appealing incentives when appropriate or deserved.
- There can be more — much more — to an incentive or reward system than financial compensation. In feedback sessions, discuss the sorts of incentives or rewards that the specific employee most desires or prefers. Perhaps a flexible schedule would be worth more than a dollar-figure raise.
- Don't get carried away with technology — Generation Jones appreciates the benefits of new technologies but maintains a solid perspective that keeps technology "in its proper place."

## TACTICS

- Bring big questions to the feedback session: Long-term goals, security, and late-stage career growth are all on Generation Jones' mind and should play a part in the feedback session.
- Generation Jones is also at the point where career transition may be under consideration — discuss ways in which the employee and your business can mutually benefit from such transitions, if the employee desires a change.

## FEEDBACK LOG: PETER

Anyone born in the boomer generation or before is not native to the new technology. They may well become maestros of all things digital, but it's an acquired skill, not something they grew up with.

I am part of that group, and I have a choice: I can work my butt off to learn new technologies — or I can team up with someone in Generation X or Y to work with me. I choose the latter.

While I am waiting for Emily, a brilliant and calm member of Generation Y, to deal with those aspects of the new technology that are beyond me, I outline the goals and content of the PowerPoint we will create. It includes cartoons and parts of videos embedded into the narrative.

I know the content and the experience I want to create but don't have a clue as to how to produce it — Emily does — she has been working with me for five years, and we work great as a team.

Today we create a speech-PowerPoint experience for a meeting of all the CEOs in the Goodwill International system throughout the U.S. and Canada — a savvy group of people who have seen it all — and our goal is to engage them in a potentially transformational experience.

The idea from a feedback perspective is to think about putting boomers and other technology-limited types in teams where the generations become a plus, not a minus. The combination of generations for a specific purpose can also produce large results and sharp insights in other, non-technical areas, as well as being challenging and fun.

For the record — and to the benefit of companies using this team approach — notice that the PowerPoint I mention was created by me and Emily. Younger team members are full members of the creative and business team — not just IT specialists or "computer geeks."

We is a powerful cross-generational term, and it's a vital concept for cross-generational feedback.

Peter

# BABY BOOMERS —
## STILL CHANGING AFTER ALL THESE YEARS

Formerly thought of as comprising 46- to 64-year-olds, boomers have been separated by recent research into two groups: Generation Jones and the group now identified as Baby Boomers. Born between the mid-1940s and the mid-1950s, these are the true-blue baby boomers. This is the generation that came of age in the '60s and early '70s during the Vietnam War, the first generation that was raised on television and listened to rock 'n' roll (to the chagrin of many of their parents). Think The Beatles, Woodstock, the first man on the moon, and the explosion of major social movements including civil rights, women's rights, and anti-war protests, and you'll have a good sense of the formative years of this group.

Social causes remain paramount to this generation — but don't make any snap judgments here, either. Woodstock Nation inspired as many (maybe more) members of this generation to oppose it as to embrace it. Just take a look at the range of political and social views held by the members of the boomer generation who run for office these days!

You'll find a lot of diversity beyond politics within this demographic group. Baby boomers include Bill and Hillary Clinton, George W. Bush, Mitt Romney, Steve Jobs, and Bill Gates, as well as Steven Spielberg, Linda Ronstadt, and Sylvester Stallone. What do these individuals have in common other than being famous and financially well-off? They're movers, shakers, and innovators. And they are all boomers.

Adjectives that describe the boomers include:

- **Individualistic** — They like to do their own thing, develop their own ideas, and create their own lives instead of following the crowd.
- **Socially Conscious** — Genuinely concerned about people's welfare, they have a deep desire, almost a sense of duty to be there for others.
- **Trendsetting** — This group tends to be innovative, creative, and not afraid to try new ways of doing things; they're definitely not into "business as usual."

- **Staying Power** — Many of the movements embraced by boomers are still going strong today.
- **Not Afraid to Experiment** — Rather than just accept what others say, they like to see for themselves and experience first-hand.
- **Innovative** — This is a natural extension of being trendsetting and individualistic.

What can you expect from a fifty- to sixty-something boomer during a feedback session? Probably an interesting exchange of ideas. Pay careful attention, because you're bound to get as many great ideas as you give out. Feedback sessions with this generation can be great for brainstorming.

Also be ready to hear about areas that need improvement from you — with the department, the company, your management style, company benefits, morale, corporate culture, social outreach, you name it. These guys are about finding real solutions, not just covering problems up with a Band-Aid. They probably won't hesitate to point out any unfair treatment, whether of themselves or their colleagues. Be prepared to be a good listener.

As with the Jones Generation, fifty- to sixty-somethings aren't necessarily looking toward retirement just yet, and they may have unconventional ideas about the whole concept. If they really love what they're doing at work, they're going to want to remain aboard well past traditional retirement ages or points, but perhaps to do so on a scaled-back basis. Stay open to the possibility of keeping them on, maybe as part-timers or consultants. Think outside the box and be open to alternative work arrangements. It very well could be to your benefit to keep this boomer on your team — with his or her wealth of experience and knowledge, this person's a good resource to keep tapping into.

Baby boomers want to reach big goals before they'll even consider their retirement years. During a feedback session, find out what these goals are. Are they hoping to become a project or team leader? A manager? Is the track they're on the one they want to stay on? Ask many questions to learn how to keep your direct reports happy and productive doing what they really want to be doing.

As with any generation, be courteous. Every time you talk with a fifty- to sixty-something about an area that needs improvement, balance it out by pointing out several things this person does well. In turn, listen carefully to what the other person has to say. And follow through on any action items you come up with during your feedback session.

# TIPS, TOOLS, & TACTICS: BABY BOOMERS

### TIPS

- Boomers are an extraordinarily diverse group. As with all other generations, don't lump all your boomer employees into a single cluster.
- Boomers are willing and even eager to experiment, and their age and work experience make it likely that their experiments will be both innovative and practical — tailor your feedback to invite their creativity.
- Big goals are vitally important to boomers, who are eager to make sure that they have "made their mark" — your feedback sessions should be aimed at determining what the employee's large, as well as near- and short-term, goals should be.

### TOOLS

- Despite boomers' comfort levels with technology, some may prefer to have paper copies of feedback materials as well as digital ones.

### TACTICS

- Retirement — or, in challenging economic times, financial security — is beginning to be much on the boomers' minds; feedback sessions should include acknowledgment of big picture planning and strategizing as well as short- or near-term goals.
- Boomers have reached the point in their lives where family responsibilities and obligations are changing, often in dramatic ways. Tuition and other expenses associated with college-aged children along with caring for aging parents are topics that may affect boomers' goals, and these should be discussed honestly and tactfully in feedback sessions.

- Give the employee the floor and listen to what she or he has to say — boomers have both opinions and the experience to back up their opinions, and their comments during feedback sessions can be invaluable for both the employee and your business.

## THE VETERAN GENERATION — I CAN'T QUIT NOW!

If you were born before 1942, you're a member of this generation.

If you were born after 1942, you grew up and have lived in a world that was shaped by the veteran generation. Their effect is still being felt. And many of them are still engaged with productive careers.

Veterans — whether literally military veterans or not — grew up in the shadows of the Great Depression, fought a world war or saw their parents fight it, became the most educated generation in history (up to that time), built the strongest economy the world had ever seen, put humans on the moon.

It's true that many in this age group are already retired, but it's also true that a large number have chosen to remain on the job. Or, crucially, been forced by economic circumstances to remain in the workforce longer — and perhaps far longer — than they had ever planned or, certainly, dreamed.

Chances are, you'll be reporting to this person, not the other way around. But not always. In addition to those who continue working as a consequence of economic circumstances, some among the 65 and older crowd have no desire to be a manager or team leader. They'd much rather work directly on a task or project than lead a team. They like designing the computer boards, making the sale, developing the procedure, working in the lab, doing the research, rolling up their sleeves and getting their hands dirty. These are the experts in their fields, the ones everyone turns to for answers. Treat them well — if they want to hang around, you'll probably want to keep them. They're valuable resources.

This group was born before 1942. Part of the Silent Generation, many were too young to remember WWII but not too young to feel its impact in major ways. The older among them may remember the late years of the Great Depression. Here's where the seeds were planted for many of the social movements that lay just around the corner as they moved from childhood into adolescence. As this generation began rising through the ranks of business, politics, and institutions, they extended and broadened reforms and changes that had been building for decades. They became seekers, and in their searches they introduced or developed many of the ideas that ultimately boomers ran with.

Terms that describe the Veteran Generation include:

- **Sensitive** — War and financial hardships left their imprints on this generation early on, makingthem somewhat less carefree and more sensitive than subsequent generations.
- **Thoughtful** — Not known for being impulsive, they like to think before they act.
- **Loyal** — They liked security and tended to marry early; many subscribe to the concept of company loyalty.
- **Seekers** — They embrace traditional ideas, to a degree, but they also seek better ways of doing things.
- **Hard Workers** — These industrious folks collectively made great strides in science, technology, business, the arts, and the early phases of key social movements.
- **Polite** — They're naturally courteous and like being treated that way.
- **Value Relationships** — Long-term, deep friendships are important to most Veterans.

The number-one rule you need to remember when giving and getting feedback with this group is respect. These folks were raised on "treat others as yourself," and they'll expect you to do the same. They may be quieter than their younger colleagues, but if you give them the chance, they'll have a lot of valuable ideas to share with you.

## FEEDBACK LOG: PETER

When 90-year-old John Glenn, still revered as the first American to orbit the earth, sold the airplane he'd owned for more than 30 years, it was all too easy to assume that the decision was made because, at his age, he couldn't pilot an aircraft anymore.

Far from it! As Glenn pointed out to NPR:

"I still have my license, and I can still pass a flight physical. But we had an airplane, a Beechcraft Baron that we — I had since 1981. And Annie and I both have had to have knee replacements, unfortunately, over the past year, and it made it more difficult for us to climb up on the airplane. We weren't using it that much, so we did — it hurt a lot, but I finally sold the airplane. But I still love to fly, and I'll never get over that."

A nice reminder that while age imposes some reconsiderations of activities and abilities, it doesn't affect *all* of them.

Peter

To the Veterans, relationships are important, and cultivating and keeping them is what they do. So don't make the mistake of treating somebody within this group like any Joe or Jane — treat him or her like a long-cherished friend. As with any generation, give them a warm handshake. Look them in the eye. Ask how things are going outside of work. Ask about family members, especially grandkids. Get to know this person on a deeper level.

But always bear in mind:

*Respect is never condescending.*

That sounds self-evident, and in an ideal world it would be, but our world is far from ideal. Even a quick look at how members of the

Veteran Generation are all too often approached will give you some insights into the negative feedback they're receiving, almost always unwittingly:

- Words like "elder" and "senior" can have positive qualities, but mostly they serve to focus attention on chronology rather than quality.
- The number of candles on a birthday cake has little to do with a person's hearing. Yet how often do we notice people raising their voices as though a Veteran must be hard of hearing?
- If a Veteran is still working, she or he is obviously still sharp — no need to simplify your language and no excuse for talking in a singsong voice as though to a child.

Someone in this age group who's still working for you is probably a solid worker, reliable, and dependable. During feedback, they'll want to know what a good job they're doing. They'll want you to point out specific ways they've helped the company. They want to feel valuable. Don't be shy about saying "thank you." Show genuine appreciation for their efforts and contributions.

And they probably won't like it if you rush through a feedback session. They'll want to listen carefully and let it all sink in. So allocate a little extra time for a session with this person. Don't keep an eye on the clock. Give your full attention to him or her. If your session goes overboard, that's OK.

Realistically, this person may not be at your company for any longer than another five or 10 years. They've worked hard their whole lives. They want to know they've accomplished something, made a difference. Don't hold back — let them know how valuable they've been and how valuable they still are. Appreciation is the operative word here.

That's especially true when, as may happen, the older employee begins to "hit the wall" of aging. Noticeable diminishment of ability — or, more seriously, mental capacity — presents a large feedback challenge, one that must be approached and handled quickly (particularly if the diminishment puts the employee or other employees at risk) but also tactfully, gracefully, and above all appreciatively. (Not to mention carefully — you are taking care of an employee's challenges, not committing even a hint of age-discrimination.)

# TIPS, TOOLS, & TACTICS: THE VETERAN GENERATION

## TIPS

- Be aware that 65+ feedback recipients are aware that they are in the latter stages of their careers.
- While I'm frequently amazed at how physically vigorous many people past 65 are, and how insightful their thoughts are, I'm also aware that this isn't true of everyone. People past 65 simply do not have the endless supplies of physical energy they possessed when younger — no matter how much they think they do.
- Don't raise your voice or simplify your language because of the feedback recipient's age — don't condescend.

## TOOLS

- Many over-sixty-fivers are uncomfortable or even wary and anxious about new technologies; as with boomers, consider teaming them with younger, more tech-savvy employees to the benefit of both.

## TACTICS

- Over-sixty-five employees are chronologically, if nothing else, in the latter stages of their careers; your awareness of this, handled gracefully and tactfully in your feedback, will help ease any concerns they fear about being "put out to pasture."
- Should an over-sixty-five employee's age begin to affect her or his ability to perform a job or fulfill responsibilities, your feedback should be honest and at the same time delicate — can you find another function the employee can fulfill? The challenge is to maintain the employee's self-respect — and value to the company — without jeopardizing the business or, far more importantly, the employee's safety and health.

# WHAT GENERATION GAP?

The best way to bridge — or eliminate — generation gaps, whether real or perceived, is to bring the generations together as much as possible, depending upon the generational composition of your team.

Cross-generational teams will likely embrace a wide range of the thinking and behavioral styles we examined in the Emergenetics section of Chapter Four. And you can, of course, shape the team be sure it embraces different styles of thinking as well as different ages.

Cross-generational teams are almost *de facto* Feedback Factories; regularly maintained and encouraged, they will become for-real Feedback Factories in no time.

Here are just a couple of general examples of feedback that flows easily through cross-generational teams.

- Older members can show the younger ones the "ropes" — their experience becomes a living thing in cross-generational teams.
- Younger members who are more comfortable with technology can both show the older teammates how to use some of the new tools and, if your structure permits this, take some of the technology-related work (and the pressure older employees sometimes feel when confronted with new digital tools) off the older members' hands.

A FEEDBACK CULTURE
  EQUALS
    GENERATION FEEDBACK,
WHICH
  GENERATES
    **GREAT FEEDBACK!**

*All media are extensions of some human faculty —psychic or physical. The wheel is an extension of the foot; the book is an extension of the eye, clothing, an extension of the skin, electric circuitry, an extension of the central nervous system.*

Marshall McLuhan,
*The Medium Is the Message*

*I tweet, therefore I am.*

Peter

*Got your e-mail, thanks.*

## CHAPTER SIX

## PUTTING WORDS INTO FEEDBACK – IN WRITING OR SPEAKING THEM

In this chapter and the next, we're going to look at the leading media or technologies for delivering feedback, everything from face-to-face conversations to instant messages and social media.

Each offers advantages and challenges, opportunities and adjustments.

Let's start with the one we're most familiar with, the personal, in-person conversation.

### FACE-TO-FACE FEEDBACK

Obviously the oldest of all forms of human communication, in-person, spoken conversation, is so common — How many people do you speak with every day? Every hour? We take it for granted. And in doing so, we overlook many aspects of spoken communication that have a direct bearing on our feedback and its effectiveness.

There's a good example on our television screens every four years. Think of the difference between the impression you get of presidential candidates from their commercials, and from their performances in face-to-face debates. This has nothing to do with politics and everything to do with how people communicate *with* each other rather than *at* each other.

A person-to-person, face-to-face feedback session, for instance, offers a variety of factors and appeals to the senses that accompany and can enhance the feedback itself:

- Tone of voice
- Facial expression and demeanor
- Physical presence and body language
- Setting and location

You will use every one of these as you deliver your feedback, whether you are consciously aware of their use or not.

And if you *are* consciously aware of these elements, you can tailor each of them to suit the specific feedback you're delivering:

- Are you smiling — or not?
- Are you standing over the employee — or seated across a table in a pleasant restaurant?
- Is your voice filled with enthusiasm and energy (or raising your voice for emphasis) — or are you deliberately flattening your tone, making clear that the feedback is being delivered in an emotionless manner?

And of course you will be "reading" your employee's or teammate's reactions by way of her or his own facial expressions, demeanor, body language, tone of voice.

Shakespeare said, "There's no art to find the mind's construction in the face," but there is some science to help us out.

## EMPATHY AND BODY LANGUAGE: THE DUCHENNE SMILE

Smile and the world smiles with you, the old saying goes.

And those smiles from around the globe will be much like yours!

The facial expression of emotions is as close to a universal language as anything is ever likely to be, as numerous researchers, from Charles Darwin in the 19th century to Paul Ekman today, have found.

French neurologist Guillaume-Benjamin-Amand Duchenne (de Boulogne), for instance, pointed out in the 19th century that the emotion of joy calls upon a combination of muscle contractions of the "zygomaticus major" muscle (lips) and the "orbicularis oculi" muscle (eyes.) In honor of its discoverer, this is called a Duchenne smile.

A Duchenne smile is a *real* smile — and its genuineness can't be faked. Which is worth keeping in mind when delivering feedback — or having any other person-to-person conversation.

You can easily fake the lip muscles (a fake smile) but not the eye muscles. If the eyes aren't "smiling," there's little joy in the other person's heart and mind, whatever is on her or his lips. (The fake smile might be referred to as the Nixon smile.) You can will your mouth to smile; you can't will your *eyes* to smile, no matter how hard you try.

Attentive managers keep their eyes on the eyes.

The more you learn about emotions and their reflection through the facial muscles, the more you'll realize that paying attention to the eyes is far more revealing than concentrating on body language, though posture is very important.

There's plenty of good information available on this subject, should you wish to learn more. I found *Emotions Revealed*, by Paul Ekman, Ph.D, to be a rich source of insight and specific advice.

And if you want to go back to the beginnings of this sort of research, take a look at *The Expression of the Emotions in Man and Animals*, by no less an observer of species than Charles Darwin. You'll never look at another person, or a pet, or, for that matter, yourself in the mirror, the same way again!

You get the idea — we all do. Person-to-person spoken conversation has been for most of our species' history *the* standard medium for communication, feedback included. So standard that we often don't give our spoken communications styles the amount of thought they deserve. The more important the feedback, the more you prepare and visualize how you're going to give it.

Now let's look at how technology changes things — and how you can adjust your feedback to take appropriate advantage of each medium's strengths.

## FEEDBACK OVER THE PHONE: HONE YOUR PHONE ZONE

Because the telephone is the extension of the voice and the ear, it immediately removes physical presence and facial expression/demeanor from the array of tools at your disposal. (The increasing availability of video calls and conference calls, and tools such as FaceTime, brings back facial expression, to an extent, but for the moment let's consider voice-only calls.)

Your phone-delivered feedback rests solely upon your voice and its qualities: You cannot add a raised eyebrow, a frown, a wink, or a pat on the shoulder; you must communicate these qualities verbally.

(We've all seen those movie and television moments when someone is saying something in one way during a telephone conversation, while at the same time mugging shamelessly in ways that are the opposite of the message being delivered. This is generally done for comic effect, but there's also more than a grain of truth in such scenes. We've all done it, and we've all been lucky that we haven't been caught at it.)

Additionally, the telephone eliminates location and setting — you, or the employee, may be in an office, at home, in the car, an airport gate area, anywhere there's a telephone connection. You could be in business garb or your pajamas, and the same goes for your employee.

You or the direct report may be dealing with distractions during the call. (And if you're making, or taking, the call while driving, you may find yourself dealing with a ticket — or worse — as a result of violating local ordnances.)

Because of these factors, telephone-delivered feedback requires adapting the basic person-to-person feedback skills to the medium you'll use. As with all feedback, you will:

- Put on your own oxygen mask first. Then:
  - ✧ Find your phone Feedback Zone.
    - For me, that means having a fresh glass of ice water to sip during the conversation; for you, it may be a cup of coffee — you'll have your own tools and talisman to make your phone time comfortable and productive.
    - Make sure your voice is strong and clear — for me, this means doing my best to avoid calls before 9 in the morning!
    - Are you relaxed and ready to laugh?
      - Wit and humor play large parts in effective communication — and thus should play large parts in your phone feedback preparation and delivery.
  - ✧ Prepare your message.
    - Key-points checklists and other necessary information should be organized and easily accessed.
      - As I point out in my training programs, if your materials are disorganized, your phone calls are likely to be the same.
  - ✧ Put first calls second.
    - Your most important calls should almost never be among your first calls of the day; making a couple of warmup calls first is akin to a baseball player's time in the on-deck circle — when you "step up to the plate," your voice and phone manner are warmed up and you're ready to "swing for the fences."
  - ✧ Be specific and precise.
  - ✧ Provide more positives than negatives.

*Then,* you will need to prepare yourself to deliver your message solely through your voice.

Can you:

- Smile — or frown — using only your voice?

- Use vocal inflection and tone to communicate nuance beyond the words you are speaking?
- Keep the person on the opposite end of the call focused on the matters being discussed?
- Know how to *listen* during a telephone conversation?
- Understand the importance of the occasional pause during a phone conversation?
    ◇ Take a second and pause.

    I remember the famous line that Jack Benny (the old-time radio comedian who was the cheapest of cheapskates) uttered to a robber who accosted him on the street with a gun and demanded "your money or your life."
    There was a long pause before Jack Benny responded, "I'm thinking, I'm thinking..."
    Great comedians, like good phone people, know the incredible value of a pause.
- Close a telephone conversation with the same positive tone that you would bring to a person-to-person meeting?

All of these skills can be refined; and for the sake of increasing the effectiveness of your feedback, all of them can benefit from regular attention, practice, and exercise.

- Practice your phone feedback technique with a recorder: Do *you* hear the qualities in your voice that you wish the employee to hear? If not, work on your tone of voice until you do.
    ◇ Call a friend or family member and practice your tone of voice. Don't forget to ask for feedback!
- Eliminate distractions in your own phone environment — and request that the employee do the same.
- If possible, avoid giving phone feedback while driving (for safety as well as clarity of feedback reasons).
- Consider adding an element to your closing in which you will review the employee's understanding of the feedback to ensure that your *meaning* and *intent* were accurately heard, as well as your words.

In short, as pointed out above, you need to put yourself in a special and specific phone *Feedback Zone*.

# INTERLUDE

## COLLABORATION DOESN'T MEAN CONSENSUS... DON'T BE A FEEDBACK COWARD

In his breakout book, *Never Eat Alone*, Keith Ferrazzi talks about building your business one relationship at a time. Former CMO at Deloitte Consulting and now with his own firm, Ferrazzi Greenlight, Keith talks in each of his books (the second is *Who's Got Your Back?*) of people and conversations as being the key to success.

Understanding how to live more in the spirit of generosity and gratitude is far more important than exchanging business cards with the hope that they can do something for you. It's them first, not you.

In building relationships, try to achieve conversations that somehow reveal people's uniqueness, which can seldom be achieved in less than a face-to-face meeting.

The question is, how can that be done with virtual teams when you're using Skype or email? Keith and his team at Ferrazzi Greenlight

*Keith Farrazzi*

have spent two years of research looking into that topic. A partial answer seems to be adding time at the beginning of the virtual meeting for "small talk," which is built in automatically in face-to-face meetings, but is left out with conference calls and video or Skype conferences.

In conference calls or Webinars, there is no time for "Harriet, how are the kids?" or "What project are you working on?" No exchanging of new and important information like the article you just read in *The Wall Street Journal* that morning that has context for this meeting.

Small talk puts the "reptilian brain" at ease, diminishes the effects of the "fight-or-flight response," and opens participants up to say more of what they're really thinking.

Keith Ferrazzi and Barbara Frederickson, Director of The Positive Emotions and Psychophysiology Lab at the University of North Carolina, talk the same language when considering the importance of how to be more "mindful" before diving into discussions or meetings in person or using technology. You have to be ready, curious, and positive, especially before a potentially tough discussion.

Barbara Frederickson

Barbara Frederickson, Ph.D, author of *Positivity* and *Love: 2.0*, has done original research on her "broaden and build" theory of positive emotions.

Her research shows that, just as negative emotions make your brain more rigid (fight or flight), "positive emotions open you up: your outlook, quite literally expands...you see more as your vision widens...you become more flexible, attuned to others, creative and wise."

The research on "face-to-face" feedback and the power to connect centers on the eyes, the smile, and the voice, which leads to "conscious feeling states," where true understanding takes place.

Recent developments in neuroscience have helped us understand why outstanding coaches and many business leaders develop great teams. They pay attention to the words they use, to looking people in the eye, and listening. To paraphrase Tom Peters, in the world of technology, face-to-face is king. (Ask Bill Clinton, one of the most influential people in the world, who is an artist at face-to-face.)

Most important for leaders is to remember that your moods are transferred to your face and into other people via what many scientists believe are "mirror neurons."

Mirror networks, located in the frontal cortex and parietal lobe of the brain, are being studied to help us understand why actions or emotions are contagious — why a parent can smile or laugh and change a crying baby into a happy one.

How can a coach take a slumping team and turn it into a winner by exuding positive emotions and upward arm motions? Because an individual or team "mirrors" those actions and emotions automatically, and goes from a slump to "catch-fire."

"We become what we behold," says Marshall McLuhan. Are you exhibiting the energy and positive emotions through your feedback that set the tone for the positive and energetic change you desire?

# MY OFFICE AS A TV STAGE-SET

The proliferation of camera-equipped phones, tablets, computers, and other devices has added a new — though long-promised — wrinkle (if you'll pardon the expression) to telephone conversations, including providing feedback over the phone.

Skype and other video calling/video conferencing technologies bring you closer to person-to-person conversation than any previous approach to what were once called "picture phones."

How does this affect delivering feedback over the phone?

For one thing, you're now re-armed with all the tools of facial expression that can enhance and extend the meaning of your words.

For another, it means that you have to be *ready* to be *seen* while you speak.

(There have been plenty of cynical comments over the years involving negative reactions to potential video phone technology: "I don't *want* a video phone! I'm *happy* doing phone business in my bathrobe!" and "You mean I have to comb my *hair* before I make a phone call?" are two that stand out.)

First — yes, you probably should comb your hair and put on something more businesslike than your robe.

Second — you need to give some thought to the setting for your video calls.

Take a good look at your current phone setting. For many of you, that will be your office and desk.

- How visually attractive and relaxing is the setting?
- What's the lighting like? Harsh and industrial — or soft and welcoming?
- Will the camera capturing your image also be capturing distractions — or embarrassments — on the wall behind you?

Adding video capability to your calls also calls upon you to address these issues. Consider:

- Review video of yourself on the phone or device you will be using. See yourself the way your direct reports will, and invest in gentle, relaxing lighting if necessary. (You should be reasonably happy with how you look...you are a big part of the message.)

- Look at what the call participant will be seeing as well as your face. Is your desk presentable, if it shows up on the screen? Is there duct tape holding together the shoulder pads or arm rests of your office chair?
- Remove clutter and hang non-distracting materials on the wall behind you. Or do the opposite, depending on the effect you want to create.

If you have the space, and if it makes practical sense, set aside a corner of your office specifically for video calls:

- Choose a neutral background.
- Arrange and adjust lighting to relax the setting's "mood."
- Provide a small table or desk on which to rest needed materials that would otherwise be on your main workspace.

Once you've established or created the ideal "set" for video calls, remind yourself of the rules that make for effective telephone feedback — and effective person-to-person feedback — and you're ready to roll camera!

## MAKING TIME FOR SMALL TALK: WEB CONFERENCING

The popularity of Internet-enabled conferences is understandable: Using Web conferencing platforms, participants in different locations are able to see the same visuals on their screens and monitors. There are dozens of such programs, each with its champions. Most such programs offer online demonstrations or sample/trial packages: Test some of them out and see which best suits your own methods and needs.

For larger companies, the decision may be made for you, of course, with the Web conferencing platform decision already in place. But you will still be able to adapt your own feedback procedures and processes to the company's choice.

While Web conferencing platforms include video calls among the services offered, my emphasis here is on the use of visuals and graphics in Web conferences. If you have video-call enabled, the same person-to-person feedback rules and tips apply.

I don't always use video during Web conferences, for a pretty simple, practical reason:

- By keeping the conference focused on the visual information and your spoken walk-through and explanation of it, you make sure your audience's focus is on the material. When I do appear in a video presentation, I am careful to keep my focus on the information as well, participating in the experience the audience is having as well as presenting it.

You may feel differently, of course. As with all the approaches to feedback in this book, and certainly with each feedback medium, you will find what best suits your own management and feedback style, which may or may not involve Web conferences (or emoticons, for that matter!).

Used effectively, Web conferencing platforms provide several opportunities:

- Deliver graphical, visual, and video information to an audience without gathering everyone in the same conference room or, for large groups and Webinars, auditorium.
- Create a log of the conference, suitable for later review.
- Easily manage the questions and comments — and feedback — from the audience: By muting audience members' voice input, I make certain that their questions and comments are entered as text, taking their place in sequence, in a queue for all participants to see.
- Because the conference takes place over the Web, it is relatively simple to bring in outside resources — Web pages that serve as examples of the point you're making, for instance — to further enhance your presentation and its effectiveness.
- Get your blood flowing first — and don't make this your first call of the day.

Your preparation for the actual feedback being delivered in the conference follows the same path and attends to the same details that any medium, and indeed any feedback session, requires:

- Put on your own web conference feedback oxygen mask first:
  ◇ Find your Feedback Zone.
  ◇ Exercise your voice — a Web conference shouldn't be your first call of the day.

- ◇ Make sure your materials are organized and ready for the presentation.
- ◇ Be the first in the virtual meeting — you called the conference; don't keep its participants waiting for you.
- ◇ Start on time.
- • Before that start time:
  - ◇ Rehearse your presentation.
  - ◇ Review your materials and ensure that all slides are clear and in the proper sequence, all words spelled correctly, etc.
    - • Measure your presentation for positives: More positives than negatives? What's the ratio?
  - ◇ Arrange for any "extras" *before* the conference starts — don't waste conference time searching for something not directly a part of your presentation but germane to it; have it on hand, to be used or not, depending on the flow of the conference.
    - • For instance, I find it helpful to have a couple of relevant cartoons ready for introduction into the conference when the time is right; before the conference starts I make sure they — or their Web location — are available for me at a single click.

During the conference:

- • Build in an appropriate amount of time in the agenda for small talk, a few minutes upfront for all participants (unless the group is too large for this to be practical) to introduce themselves, say hello, and catch up with their news.
- • Monitor the time and keep an eye on the questions and comments box.
- • Try not to let more comments — and especially questions — queue up than available time will allow you to address.
  - ◇ Look for opportunities to combine questions and areas of comment.
  - ◇ If possible and appropriate, address each questioner and commenter by name.
- ◇ At the close of the conference, thank everyone for participating.

After the conference:

- • Ask for feedback from the participants; you can do this with a mass email (but with the personal touches we looked at above).

◇ Consider a conference feedback form or checklist — find out specifically if you did as well (or as poorly) with your audience as you thought you did, and in what areas.

• If any of the participants stood out and raised the conference to new or unexpected levels, drop them a private email or consider *mixing* the media:

◇ Even a quick handwritten note after a digital conference will stand out as "special" feedback.

## PAPER STILL HAS ITS PLACE

Now let's look at what happens when we further reduce your communications tools by eliminating voice and examining several written-only feedback media.

The "paperless office," once thought to be an inevitable consequence of the computer revolution, didn't happen.

Even if 99% of your communication is now accomplished via email, phone, and txt, you undoubtedly still find yourself dealing with a fair amount of paper related to your direct reports. Make the most of it!

Paper communications of all sorts, from forms to handwritten notes and letters, can fill a variety of feedback roles, no matter how digital the bulk of your communication becomes.

Clearly, because we have moved to a "silent" medium, paper communication places the focus — and the pressure! — on words and your use of them. Because you do not have the added sensory appeals that voice provides to phone conversations, and that physical presence delivers to person-to-person meetings, your written words, whether in the form of correspondence or commentary on forms, must represent your meaning.

In other...*words*, you must be able to write as clearly and unambiguously as you speak, adapting your feedback to a medium where written words are doing all the work. (For a good example of this economical yet interesting writing, reread Ernest Hemingway's *The Old Man and the Sea*.) This isn't as hard as it sounds. And it may not sound hard to you at all — but more and more people, in our age of constant and often instant electronic communication, have remarked that they find writing difficult. (Some have argued, in fact, that writing is no longer a necessary or "relevant" skill! They're wrong.)

# PUTTING PERSONALITY TO PAPER

Paper communications need not be dull and lack personality. Far from it. While it's true that back in the heyday of the IBM Selectric, every typewritten memo or letter looked pretty much the same, it's even more true that we're no longer in the age of the typewriter, and haven't been for quite a while.

The combination of word processing software, a good printer, and some experience — or experimentation — with various fonts, bolds and italics, spacing, and and other typographic strategies means that
your
**written**
COMMUNICATIONS
**can have a *LOT OF***
**VISUAL FLAIR AND**
PERSONALITY!!!!!

Obviously, it's easy to overdo this sort of thing — as I've just shown. As with emoticons and other special effects, a little "extra" can go a long way. But without that little extra, your written communications run the very real risk of losing some of their impact and effectiveness as a result of being simple "words on paper."

Fortunately, the steps you've taken toward establishing a solid and consistent Feedback Posture for yourself are every bit as applicable to paper (and all other feedback media) as person-to-person meetings and telephone conferences. And, as with all other feedback media, paper communication requires that you:

- Put on your own oxygen mask first.
- Find your paper Feedback Zone:
  ◇ Before writing, outline the message you need to send.
  ◇ Be specific and precise.

◇ If time permits, do a first draft that you WON'T send — then edit it on paper, making sure that every word sends the feedback message you desire.

◇ Once your message is completed to your satisfaction:
  • Read your words from the recipient's perspective: How will your direct report or teammate read your words? Any possibility for misinterpretation?
  • Above all, ask yourself:
    • What's the emotional tone I want my direct report or boss to be in after reading what I've written?
  • Revise as necessary.
    • If you're not confident that your message is completely clear and unambiguous, get a trusted advisor to read it and provide an outside opinion.

◇ Remember the importance of positivity:
  • Make sure positives outnumber negatives by by a measurable number.

◇ Adapt — where appropriate and possible — your written communications to your understanding of the recipient's brain-style and behavior style.

Above all, your paper communications should also — and, to be effective, *must* — reflect your own brainstyle, behavior style, and management style. Tailor the content to the styles of the recipient.

Bearing this in mind, give some thought to the various ways you already use paper to provide feedback — and ways that you could add paper tools to your feedback arsenal:

• Forms and checklists: These may be more a matter of your company's policy and structure than your own preferences; if so, attach a handwritten feedback-related note to forms before sending to the direct report.

• Don't overlook the special benefits derived from handwritten notes and messages — more personal than computer printouts of written material, feedback captured in your "hand" can carry extra weight and is immediately recognizable as a personal communiqué.

• Consider dropping the occasional greeting card to direct reports or clients, with handwritten feedback inside.

- When composing your written materials on a computer or tablet, proofread the results carefully before printing and sending. Typos and grammatical errors send messages too — but not good ones.

Don't forget that paper is a perfect medium for building your personal brand. In addition to letterhead, consider making a small investment in special materials that can give your feedback special impact:

- Sources such as The Cartoon Bank (**http://cartoonbank.com**) offer the opportunity to buy cartoons for your own use; find one that suits your management style and the message you want to send, buy it and have cards printed up that can be mailed out as needed.
- Don't forget — or neglect — the fact that paper is *tactile*. For special correspondence, consider special paper to help the message stand out and "touch" the direct report.
- Printed (brief) newsletters remain effective even in this age of blogs and other online news sources. Design and print up a newsletter for your team — fill it with the sorts of general but valuable feedback that's worth sharing and deserves repeating.
  ✧ Invite your team members to submit items to the newsletter.
  ✧ I always advise against buying pre-written newsletters. You know the kind of thing I'm talking about: a page or four of "canned" articles and nuggets of humor and wisdom (which generally prove to be neither), with a few blank spaces in which you insert your own material. What do you generally do with such material? If you answer the way I do, you — and your wastebasket — have just made my point.

## FEEDBACK LOG: PETER

One of my most interesting projects had as much to do with what I learned as with what advice and help I gave. I worked as a consultant to Sharp Healthcare of San Diego, one of the nation's larger healthcare companies. My time was spent mostly with a CEO and her C-level executives. We spent our efforts on peak performance and health for her managers, and on coaching and feedback as a follow-up.

She was prompt at giving verbal feedback, but she also had a very different and creative way of using paper (as in greeting cards, both specific and general — and some outrageously humorous). She kept a large supply of greeting cards in the closet of her office; when she wanted to drop a bit of unexpected feedback to a direct report, or any of her 400 employees, she had an appropriate card on which to do so.

She called it her "Closet of Planned Spontaneity."

This closet served two purposes. First, she had something ready for any unexpected occasion; and secondly, her raids on the greeting card sections of grocery stores, especially during stressful times, kept her in humorous spirits. Paper isn't dead as a means of feedback...it's all in how you use it.

Peter

# TIPS, TOOLS, & TACTICS

TIP: If possible with face-to-face feedback, pick a pleasant, neutral location or setting. The fewer external distractions, the more closely you will be able to focus on the matters at hand.

TIP: Keep a glass of water or a cup of tea close by when making a feedback-related phone call; make sure your voice remains clear and strong.

TIP: Don't underestimate — or overlook — the value of a handwritten note or greeting card. Make sure your handwriting is legible.

TOOL: Have someone take a video as you practice a face-to-face feedback session. Watch the video and correct anything that strikes you as off-center or less than effective. Repeat the exercise as necessary, while taking care to keep your presentation from becoming "canned."

TOOL: If you are using a headset or mobile phone, invest in the best technology. Your phone presence is important and shouldn't be undercut by low-quality microphones or connections.

TOOL: Paper still has a place — an important one! There are definite advantages to paper media, which include:

• Stationery

• Greeting cards

• Post cards

• Printed newsletters (but only if they've got something to say!)

TACTIC: Remember that physical presence — whether you're standing or sitting, proximity to your feedback recipient, etc. — plays a role in face-to-face conversations. Make sure your body language sends the same message as your words.

TACTIC: A feedback-related phone call — any important phone call, in fact — should never be your first call of the day. Give yourself and your voice a brief, less consequential workout first.

TACTIC: When you're feeling anxiety, be sure to breathe deeply from your diaphragm, rather than your chest. Deep diaphragmatic breathing eases anxiety.

*Technology is
anything that wasn't around
when you were born.*

**computer scientist Alan Kay**

*No, the computers are up, we're down.*

## CHAPTER SEVEN

## VIRTUAL FEEDBACK

The first time I received an email with a ☺ next to her congratulations for a particularly nice piece of news, my own face matched the image on the screen.

The sender had found a way — familiar to us all by now — to add a little extra "personality" to her email, to enrich and extend, however slightly, her positive message to me. I appreciated it.

If, on the other hand, all I'd received from her had been the emoticon alone, a smile without context, as it were, I might have been as puzzled as I was pleased.

But my correspondent knew instinctively — emoticons were brand-new then; nobody had a lot of experience with them — that a small ☺ placed in proximity to a large piece of good news would communicate her own pleased smile, along with the written congratulations it accompanied.

Emoticons are everywhere today, and while they have lost their novelty, they haven't lost their effectiveness (except for those people who *over*-use them! ☹!).

One of the reasons that emoticons such as ☺ ("smiley") or ☹ ("frowny"), along with their elaborate, colorful, and often animated companions, have grown so popular and ubiquitous is precisely that they *aren't* specific: Their message, and purpose, is simple:

- This made me smile.
- This made me frown.

Appending that message to a more detailed written message is equally simple, and offers a good example of how a little "extra" feedback can put a human "face" on a communication that might come across as dry or flat.

And emoticons are only one element of the technological universe that's transformed our workplaces and our society.

We'll come back to emoticons later in this chapter, after we take a larger look at the opportunities — and challenges — that technology can present to a growing Feedback Culture.

# THE TECHNOLOGY JUGGERNAUT

Technology changes almost everything.

And digital technology changes almost everything *fast*.

Rather than letting technology change the nature of your feedback, you should be alert for the many ways you can transform *technology* into a feedback engine.

Anyone who's experienced even a brief interruption in electric power services understands just how pervasive information and communications technologies have become in a relatively short time, as well as how pervasive our dependence upon technology and expectation of constant access to it have become in consequence. Think about what the past 30 or so years have brought:

PCs and Macs, BlackBerrys, smartphones, iPads and other tablets, broadband and wireless access, along with email, txtng (I'll use the medium's conventions when referring to it), instant messaging, Web pages, blogs, Facebook, Twitter, LinkedIn, and, yes, even the emoticons and other special effects they enable have transformed the workplace at every level.

One consequence of this transformation has been a real shift in the nature of our presence among widespread employees and far-flung offices and facilities.

Where once we might have scheduled regular quarterly person-to-person meetings with distant direct reports, and supported those with weekly phone calls, email and related technologies enable us to be in constant touch in ways that even the phone did not.

While the telephone made more frequent contact among distant offices and employees possible — and still does, as the Polo/Ralph Lauren example in Chapter Two showed — the phone offered only a hint of how constant (to the point of being sometimes overwhelming) newer communications technologies would be.

Nor did relatively stable telephone technologies — the shift from dial phones to push-buttons was considered a major change in its day — prepare us for the equally constant wave of upgrades, improvements, new generations, and whole new types of technologies we've experienced for the last third of a century.

In some ways I'm reminded of *The Sorcerer's Apprentice*, wherein a magical spell grows so chaotically out of control that Mickey Mouse is spending all of his time and energy trying to keep up with its consequences.

So what does all of this have to do with feedback?

Everything.

## THE FEEDBACK MEDIUM IS THE MESSAGE

Whatever the technology — email, Web-based forums, online chats, and so on — you use to deliver feedback to your team, it is vital to bear in mind that the *content* of the feedback is what's important, and your understanding of the various delivery media has a large ring on the effectiveness of your feedback.

The *same* piece of feedback can deliver very different messages as a result of the delivery medium you use.

Marshall McLuhan's great insight — *the medium is the message* — is particularly apt here. McLuhan's lesson that the medium itself becomes part of the message being delivered has large implications for feedback. "It is the framework that changes with each new technology and not just the picture within the frame."

Phone, paper, email, txts, instant messages, social media, even good old ink-on-paper — each medium offers advantages and constrictions for the delivery of effective feedback.

*Only by understanding the nature of the medium can you shape your feedback to take best advantage of the medium's strengths while avoiding its weaknesses.*

While they're not exactly a medium unto themselves, those ☺ and ☹ emoticons I addressed at the beginning of this chapter offer a good example.

If your feedback were to consist only of a ☺ or ☹, you would be sending a strong and, I believe, unfortunate message that includes the following signals:

- I didn't care enough to do more than click a key or two.
- You aren't worth any more time than a key click or two.
- I don't really have anything constructive to say to you on this matter other than a vague smile or frown.

None of which are of great value to the team member — quite the opposite, in fact.

That's a vastly simplified example, and quite frankly there are times when a smiley is *absolutely* the sole piece of feedback you need to send, but I hope you get the idea.

On a more sophisticated level, consider email. If your direct reports receive constant emails from you — several a day, say — you will need to develop and implement a strategy that distinguishes important feedback mail from routine business mail.

This was in many ways simpler in the world of paper communications: A FedEx envelope marked URGENT is a medium that sends an immediate message, particularly if such packages are a rarity from the sender.

An email bearing the red IMPORTANT flag — which few people, in my experience, use anyway — is unlikely to communicate the same level or degree of urgency, for a very simple reason:

- One email pretty much looks like another, particularly if the recipient's email queue receives dozens (or hundreds!) of emails a day (many of which may bear that red IMPORTANT flag, whether they are important to the recipient or not).

Does this mean you should use FedEx or another paper-based medium for your feedback? Not at all — you should use the medium that best suits you, your business, and the needs and work habits of your direct reports.

For most of us, three decades into the digital revolution, that medium will most likely be electronic: email, though your company may have introduced collaborative tools and technologies that you use for internal communications.

The point is the same, whatever the technology:

*For the purposes of creating and delivering effective feedback, you must consider the medium by which the feedback is delivered. The medium really IS the message — and the same message can be changed by the medium you use.*

Let's take a look at how the same feedback is altered by different media of virtual communication, including:

- Email
- Txt
- Social media

## EMAIL FOR HEROES AND COWARDS

Do you remember the first piece of email you ever received?

For most of us, it was a message welcoming us to the world of email, either from the manufacturer of the software we used for mail or from an employer's network administrator or your Internet service provider doing the same.

Now, do you remember the:

- First piece of *business* email you received?
- First piece of business email you *sent*?
- First piece of spam you received?
- First piece of business email that *reminded* you of spam (time-wasting, irrelevant, even ridiculous)?

- First time you felt overwhelmed by the volume of email you receive daily?
- The most recent time you took 24 hours off from checking your email on any device?

Whether or not you can answer those questions specifically, you certainly have experience with each type of email. And it's a safe bet that however long ago you received or sent your first email, the medium is now among your primary — and possibly *the* primary — means of written communication you employ.

So: How good a medium for *feedback* is email?

Depends on the type of feedback you're sending.

For follow-up and follow-through messages, building upon a foundation established in person-to-person, phone, or paper feedback, email can be quite effective, offering a variety of benefits and advantages. Email is:

- Fast
- Available on multiple platforms
- Automatically date- and time-stamped
- A more permanent record than a phone call
- A "trail" of commentary and response

Bearing these virtues in mind, let's look at the deficits of email:

- Relatively impersonal and faceless
- Easy to be hasty and imprecise when "dashing off" an email
- Easy to mis-address or mis-send an email

Of those, it is the impersonality of email that most directly affects your choice of email as a feedback medium.

Later in this section I'll take a look at some ways you can add a personal touch and "feel" to your emails, but for now let's accept the fact that one email can look pretty much like another.

Because of this "standardization" of appearance, email is not likely to be the medium of choice for major feedback presentations and conversations. Those types of feedback events are best handled person-to-person (ideally), with phone (or video conference), if available, as a second choice.

Whether the major feedback you're delivering is predominantly positive or negative, your effectiveness in communicating your precise message will be vastly enhanced by having at your disposal the tools of facial expression, tone of voice, body language, and other in-person attributes unavailable in an email.

But you wouldn't want to send negative feedback by email, anyway. At least I wouldn't. I've heard more than a few horror stories from people who've been laid off or fired in an email, and I find such stories, well, horrifying.

One of the overall themes of this book, and my seminars and training programs presenting The Feedback Revolution, is that:

• *Effective business feedback is never faceless.*

Feedback, whatever its delivery medium, should always clearly be the product of a human being. This is one of the keys to the creation of an effective Feedback Culture and, not incidentally, one of the keys to the most effective use of the various media available for delivering and receiving feedback.

With your direct reports, and colleagues with whom you are in frequent or regular contact, your emails should already be carrying a certain level of personality and personalization.

Your regular recipients know you, are accustomed to your voice and tone, and may even "hear" your voice when they read your email.

And still you should not want to send major feedback in an email: The medium simply does not offer the level of intimacy, nuance, and interplay that important feedback demands.

A good rule of thumb that's applicable to far more than email is this:

• Would *I* want to receive this news in this way?

It's more accurate to say that email isn't an effective medium for delivering or introducing *major feedback*. For follow-up and follow-through, as well as clarification and discussion, email is terrific and, because of its time/date-stamp and threading features, ideal.

# INTERLUDE

## GENERAL GEORGE S. PATTON (as played by George C. Scott) AND MARISSA MAYER: DELIVERING THE MESSAGE PROPERLY CAN BE AS IMPORTANT AS THE MESSAGE ITSELF

George S. Patton, arguably the finest battlefield commander of World War II and without argument the greatest leader of American armored troops in history, was focused on defeating the enemy ahead of him and his army. Anyone who's seen George C. Scott's brilliant portrayal of him in *Patton* will recall numerous scenes where the audacious general boldly attacked, and did so often against conventional wisdom, and even against orders from his superiors.

*General George S. Patton*

A scene in the film captures Patton's approach beautifully:

After a particularly stormy and dramatic tirade by Patton, an aide tells the general that sometimes his troops can't tell what is and isn't an act. "It's not important that they know," Patton replies. "It's only important that I *know*."

Another unforgettable scene showed Patton directing traffic as his armor moved into enemy territory. The traffic jam unsnarled, the great general walked side by side with his troops.

Patton's stagecraft was designed to deliver expectations — and his feedback — to his army in the most effective way possible: He knew what he was doing and why he did it the way he did. At least, that's the version the movie told us.

Now consider the effects of another leader seeking to rally the "troops." I'm speaking of Marissa Mayer, the young (37) CEO of Yahoo, charged with turning the once-great company around.

In one of her first leadership moves, Mayer brought an end to the company's long-standing policy of letting employees telecommute, or work from home. She made the policy change known in a company-wide email that, of course, got leaked to the press.

Judging by the firestorm of news stories, editorials, blog posts, tweets, and the rest, you would have thought that Mayer had committed the corner-office equivalent of slapping a soldier. More than a few Yahoo employees announced that they would leave the company rather than adjust to the new rules. (Those departures may have been part of Mayer's strategy as she implemented the policy change.) Debate raged over whether Mayer's announcement was a good, bad, or disastrous opening move in her tenure as Yahoo CEO.

*Marissa Mayer*

What Mayer had actually done was quite reasonable: There are dramatic and well-documented reasons to prefer that teams work in physical proximity to one another — the water-cooler effect, the opportunities for impromptu conversations, chance encounters that spark inspirations, the unexpected incident of "feedback on the fly," and more.

Besides which, *she* is the CEO, and the implementation of her vision of what's best for Yahoo is, after all, what she's being paid for.

Where Mayer made a mistake, I believe, was in *how* she delivered her vision. Email, as I discuss in the Technofeedback chapter, is an effective medium for many types of communication and feedback. But for large changes in direction, strategy, and culture, there's no substitute for in-person, face-to-face dialogue. This, it seems, would be especially obvious for a change of direction that rests upon the importance of that personal presence in the workplace.

How different the public — and more importantly the internal — response to Mayer's change in company policy might have been had she "put her face where her words were." A company-wide video address, in which the new CEO made clear her reasons for the change in policy, and her excitement over the new directions for Yahoo's culture, would have been far more effective.

Anyone who's seen *Patton* remembers the opening scene in which the general, in full battle regalia, stirringly addresses his troops, and does so by pulling no punches about the battles, and the deaths, that lie ahead.

It's a great speech — and would have made a lousy email.

# SUBJECT LINES AS MARKETING

One good way to assess the effectiveness of a feedback-related email is to pay attention to the mail's subject line.

For instance:

*Disastrous results this quarter — must discuss future*

is both a pretty clear case of "too much information" for a subject line to bear and an example of a subject line that's all too easy to misinterpret:

- Whose results were disastrous? The company's or the recipient's?
- Disastrous in what ways?
- Must discuss the future of what? While you may think it's clear that it's the *results*' effect on the next quarter that must be discussed, your direct report's immediate thought would rightly be that her or his future with the company is what's on the table.

Email subject lines, then, are a prime example of the importance of specificity, clarity, and precision.

But since the space available in a subject line is limited (a restriction we'll explore more closely in the following section on txts), it's best to craft your subject lines carefully, making sure that they communicate only as much as they need to ensure that the mail attracts the desired attention:

- Let's have a conversation tomorrow, re next quarter goals
- Can you set aside an hour to spend with me on this?

Lay the groundwork for the body of the email, in which you can make clear — being deliberate about positives outnumbering negatives — that the discussion will include:

- Agreement that the discussion will take place: you've asked permission
- A review of the current quarter
- An evaluation of positives and negatives related to quarterly performance
- A solid discussion and action plan for the upcoming quarter
- A scheduled time for the phone or person-to-person conversation

This sort of checklist can be an effective tool for preparing the body of any email. It's a way of putting on your oxygen mask first and finding your Feedback Zone *before* the feedback session takes place.

Notice as well that the checklist — and the email that contains it — is almost purely informational; you are outlining what will be discussed during the feedback session, not previewing the contents of the session.

(That said, you — like any effective manager — will be aware that any time there's a request for an unexpected conversation, the direct report's antennae — or paranoia — will go an alert. Be sure to close the email with an enthusiastic and *positive* sign-off, helping allay the team member's fears.)

One item that the recipient won't notice — except in the effectiveness of your emails — is an invariable commitment to

*Take a breath and read the email before sending it.*

It's all too easy to get in the habit of hitting the SEND button as soon as an email is composed. This is a habit that's well worth breaking. A reread, along with revising and, if necessary, rewriting the email for increased clarity and a better, more positive tone is a small investment of time that can yield large results in understanding, comprehension, and enthusiasm.

A reread also helps avoid the problem of too-quickly sending a private email to more than the desired recipient. In other words:

*PAUSE BEFORE SENDING.*

That brief opportunity to take a breath, review what you've written, and consider its accuracy and effectiveness can make the difference between "one more email" and an email filled with effective feedback.

I'll be honest — the pre-send pause is good advice, but it flies in the face of a lot of pressures.

I know someone who has taped a small sign to his monitor:

*DON'T SEND UNTIL IT'S SENDABLE!*

He swears that the effectiveness of his emails has increased at least fivefold!

The pause before sending also offers the opportunity to review the tone as well as the content of the email. A good business email to a direct report should be enthusiastic and appreciative as a face-to-face conversation. Your emails, like all of your feedback, should leave your direct report in a positive state, engaged and energized, emotionally excited about the prospects that lie ahead.

This sort of pause and review, frankly, can also be the sort of thing that fits all too easily into the "Where do you expect me to find the extra time to do that?" file.

In the second place, don't think of it as "extra" time — think of it as the right amount of time needed to do this part of your job properly. Providing effective, useful, and *usable* feedback to your direct reports is your job. You are *delegating* the time to this purpose, because the purpose is worth it.

And in the *first* place, the "extra time" you might be worried about is really only the "extra time" required to turn the pause before sending practice into *habit*, something you do as a matter of course, like putting on your own oxygen mask first and finding your Feedback Zone.

Before you know it, sending an email *without* that review, reflection, and revision will be unthinkable.

You'll appreciate that you've acquired a new habit — and so will the recipients of your email.

## THE LETTER ABRAHAM LINCOLN *DIDN'T* MAIL — SOMETIMES THE PAUSE BEFORE SENDING SHOULD BE PERMANENT!

In the aftermath of the battle of Gettysburg, Abraham Lincoln was profoundly aware of the symbolic qualities of the victory. Lee's invasion of Union territory had been turned back decisively. Never again would Southern forces drive so far into the North.

But the president was also deeply aware that the victory was more symbolic than militarily decisive. After the three days of fighting that resulted in Confederate General Pickett's doomed, disastrous charge against Union emplacements, the Union had failed to press its advantage and completely destroy the Confederate army, effectively ending the war on the fields of Pennsylvania in the summer of 1853.

By choosing instead to rest and regroup his forces after the fighting ended, Union General George Meade allowed Robert E. Lee and the surviving Confederate army to escape back into the South. Meade's caution had doomed the nation to nearly two more years of tragic, devastating war.

Lincoln penned what he referred to himself as a "stinging" letter of rebuke to Meade, making clear that the general could not even begin to comprehend his Commander in Chief's disappointment.

When he had finished writing the letter, Lincoln placed it in an envelope, sealed it, and wrote across the front:

**DO NOT SEND**

The president knew that Meade had failed to fulfill his military responsibilities, and that the failure of generalship was calamitous.

But the great president also knew that the contents of his letter, if mailed, would become public, not only muting the symbolic aspects of Gettysburg, but also sowing discontent among the military leaders whose confidence in Lincoln was shaky.

The letter served its purpose — Lincoln gave voice to his feelings and, having put those feelings into words, chose to keep them to himself.

Sometimes the best and most effective feedback is that which we *don't* communicate immediately. A fact that Lincoln may well have come to appreciate over the months following Gettysburg, during which time Meade's failures fully to engage Lees army, despite plenty of opportunities to do so, made it politically far easier for Lincoln, in March, 1864, to place Ulysses S. Grant in overall command of the Union forces, relegating Meade to a subordinate role.

Maybe we need a DO NOT SEND button to be in the most prominent place when we are writing important emails.

A word here on appreciation. A positive tone and an atmosphere of graciousness and gratitude are important elements of *all* effective email, whether feedback-related or not. All of us receive too much email, and most of it is a waste of time (even after the best email filters winnow the queue).

It is to great business benefit that *your* emails stand out by virtue not only of their contents (and the fact that you are the direct report's boss), but also because you have taken the trouble

- To give the emails a "face" by way of your word choices and personalization
- To shape the contents for clarity and specificity
- To include a higher percentage of positives than negatives
- To defer critical or distressing information for personal conversation to build in an air of gratitude and appreciation for the recipient

---

### EMAIL GETS THE VOTE

Consider having an email contest among your direct reports and team members. Have them submit their choices for the most effective email they sent this month, then share the submissions with the whole group (removing the sender's and recipients' names to make the contest fair).

The group will vote on which they feel was the month's best email, and the winner will receive a small token such as a gift card.

Once the contest ends, gather everyone together to review why the winner won, as well as the virtues of the other pieces of mail.

In other words:

*YOUR MAIL GETS FEEDBACK!*

---

I have found as well that the on-screen appearance of an email benefits from some personal aesthetic attention. Once I've written an email, I make sure that the body of the message is well-spaced, with plenty of open screen between lines, making the actual message that I send both more inviting and easier to read.

While I keep my emails pretty bare-bones in terms of effects other than line spacing, you may find it worthwhile to do some experimenting with background color, font and style, and other enhancements that lend further personality to your electronic correspondence.

In fact, you might consider working with your direct reports to design a team-specific email "look and feel" so that internal mail among members of your direct-responsibility team stand out and are instantly identifiable.

As we've seen, the neutral and even "flat" effect of email can be remedied with a little thought and effort, time and care, making email an effective vehicle for certain types of feedback.

Now, let's look at another electronic medium that's even more proscribed than email, and that requires even more careful use when it comes to feedback.

Time to TXT!

# CAN U TXT FDBK?

The easy answer is:

*NO U CANT!*

But, as we've seen with every other aspect of feedback and technology, the easy answer is rarely the *complete* answer.

Txtng — again, I'll use the medium's conventions when referring to it — is a hybrid offshoot of telephone and messaging technologies. In fact, the formal name for the technology underlying txtng is SMS — short message service — and its roots go back to the earliest days of mobile communications.

The emphasis is on *short*.

## TXT IS THE NEW TELEGRAM

The first sophisticated means of near-instantaneous communication was the telegraph. As with every major advance and evolution in communications media, the telegraph, and the medium of communication, the telegram, changed every-thing.

One thing it changed was how messages are composed. In a letter, the correspondent had as much space as needed; it is not unusual to see letters of dozens of pages in the pre-telegraph and, especially, pre-telephone days.

It was different with a telegram. Because telegraphy services charged by the word, correspondents learned quickly to be careful and economical as they composed their messages. A kind of shorthand developed, with every unnecessary word eliminated. Instead of:

*What is the status of current sales?*

for instance, a businessman might write:

*What status sales?*

Saving words meant saving money.

The shorthand could lead to misunderstandings, and humor, as in the probably apocryphal story of a reporter on a tight deadline for a feature about Cary Grant. Not knowing the actor's age — this was pre-Google and Wikipedia — he cabled:

*How old Cary Grant?*

To which the notoriously private actor immediately responded:

*Old Cary Grant fine. How you?*

The point, other than laughter, is that when we're space-limited, whether for economical reasons or by the character-count restrictions placed on txts and tweets, we have to choose carefully — but we also have to make sure the message can't be misinterpreted.

While technical evolution has stretched the limits and capabilities of txt messages and the phones and mobile devices that are used to send and receive them, brevity remains the soul of the txt.

The medium is so popular, convenient, and pervasive that laws are being enacted to restrict drivers from txtng while behind the wheel. And we've all heard stories about people sending and receiving txts to each other while seated *opposite* each other!

But popularity and convenience, and even pervasiveness, don't automatically make a medium appropriate for feedback, especially high-level feedback.

Txts *are* good for:

- Immediate and urgent material, if it can be contained in a txt
  - ✧ This is, in my opinion, the *best* use of txts –
    - The ringtone or vibration a phone gives when a txt arrives is like old-time newsboys hawking papers: EXTRA! EXTRA!
    - As a consequence, txts tend to be treated with more immediacy, even urgency, than emails
    - I *always* check a txt the moment I receive the signal that it has arrived
- Quick bursts of information
- Acknowledgments and confirmations
- Changes in schedule and other agenda items
- Quick bursts of enthusiasm and encouragement
- Brief updates and follow-throughs

Txts are *not* good for:

- Substantive or nuanced information
- Negative information or feedback
- Detailed analyses or reviews

Some of this is (or should be) self-evident, but in looking back over my logs I see that as I was growing used to txtng, I tended to treat the messages as very brief emails, replying to or acknowledging every one. One day the light bulb went off and I saw the error in my early txtng ways.

## FEEDBACK LOG : PETER

Just had a good lesson in txts from my daughter, who sent:

*On my way. B there n 20 mins.*

And that was it.

My first impulse was to txt her right back with a

*Great! I'm here!*

But a second's reflection made me see that there was no need for such a message. I was in my office and would be there 20 minutes later when Jennifer arrived.

If, on the other hand, I'd received her txt while I was away from my office, I'd have sent:

*Rnning ltl late; wait for me.*

Or something like that.

Txt is an ideal medium for brief exchanges of information.

And for brief bits of positive feedback:

• Exclnt call this morning

• Delighted wth ur sales figures

• Bravo on ur presentation!

That sort of thing.

Quick, to the point, upbeat — the kind of feedback on the fly (see Chapter 10) that makes receiving a txt another aspect of a thriving Feedback Culture.

And since it is a culture, it's worth discussing txt etiquette with your direct reports — what sorts of txts do you expect a reply to, and what types are for receipt only, no response necessary.

Peter

The shorthand abbreviations that are a part of txtng — and are becoming an accepted form of writing in general among many Millennials — have a specific purpose — they conserve limited character space, letting you pack the maximum amount of information into a short txt.

Keep that specific purpose — a txt — in mind. While the occasional LOL or even OMG, like the occasional emoticon, can be used to good effect in an email, or even in a piece of on-paper communication, for the most part txt-speak should be contained within the world of txts (IMHO, anyway).

Since txts serve a specific purpose — quick, immediate, or urgent communications — here are three specific and quick pieces of advice on txts and feedback:

---

### THREE SIMPLE RULES FOR TXTNG FEEDBACK

1. Don't txt negative feedback — save it for another medium.
2. Use txts to maintain — and extend — positive emotional states with good, quick reinforcement messages.
3. Don't feel obliged to reply to purely informational txts — and let your direct reports know that they can do the same.

---

# SOCIAL MEDIA IS *NOT* THE FEEDBACK MESSAGE

Not for internal, business-related feedback messages anyway.

For public feedback, social media (Facebook, Google+, Twitter, etc.) has proved itself to be a valuable source of *public* feedback.

Similarly, LinkedIn, the most business-oriented of social media, offers you the opportunity to post and communicate information about yourself, as well as to comment on and recommend (or not) the work of others.

Facebook's "Like" button, to pick the most obvious example, has been used to good effect as a sort of informal, limited polling tool, both for individuals and for the marketing and public relations arms of some companies.

But in addition to its clearly limited information content, the "Like" button is public. Even with the constantly refined privacy settings that social media companies roll out, there is always the risk that an internal feedback comment will be seen by people other than the person for whom it was intended.

Interestingly — and tellingly — enough, the ongoing refinement and tightening of the privacy settings for social media, search, and other software is itself a result of, you guessed it, *feedback*. Public and media outcries about just who can see what information have prodded companies to provide more and more privacy controls to their users.

But there remain multiple problems for using social media internal communications such as feedback to or from a direct report:

- Privacy settings have to be *set* by the user: You've got no guarantee that all of your direct reports will accurately reset their privacy controls. All it takes is one oversight and your carefully prepared private feedback might be seen by hundreds, even thousands, of unintended, unwanted viewers.
- Social media has suffered numerous hacks and outside incursions since its introduction. While private email and internal communications systems can be hacked, and have been, social media platforms such as Facebook are extraordinarily appealing targets because of the sheer size of the population using them. Facebook alone boasts more than 10% of the *world's* population as users.
- Even with the strictest privacy settings enabled, preventing unauthorized users from seeing information, most social media and search companies retain the right to inspect your information themselves. Generally this is done for demographic and advertising purposes, but the point is nonetheless clear — social media is no place for internal feedback.

While all of the above are good reasons to avoid using public social media for internal feedback, it remains likely that you, or at least some members of your team, will have and enjoy a Facebook, Google+, Twitter, or LinkedIn presence. Some of your direct reports and colleagues may be "power users" of such services. More power, as it were, to them! *But –*

- You need to establish clear rules about what business-related observations and comments, however innocuous on the surface, your direct reports are permitted to make on public social media sites.

Most companies of sufficient size, as well as many schools and other institutions, have already begun addressing this situation, with some going so far as to prohibit employees from having personal Facebook or other social media accounts.

I don't think you have to be that draconian, but some sharply defined rules for social media use as it relates to your internal communications are definitely in order. The easiest way to show why is to offer a few examples of Facebook postings or tweets that can have unexpected, unwanted consequences:

- Got my big performance review today! Hope the boss is in a good mood!
- Just had a great review — raise in store!
- Lousy review this morning — hate my boss!
- Boss is hung up on making us all "love feedback" — I don't — and there's no way he can make me change!

And so on.

None of these, or similar, comments are appropriate for public dissemination, especially when some of the public viewing the comments could well include other team members, whose reviews may not have gone so well. You get the picture.

Even worse in some ways — the public viewing the comment might include your superior, who's likely to give you some pointed feedback about why your direct reports are posting internal, supposedly confidential information on Facebook.

Human nature all but guarantees that you're not going to keep direct reports and colleagues from discussing internal matters among themselves. Call it the "Water Cooler Effect."

The difference is that Facebook and other social media water coolers draw crowds of thousands — or more. The solution:

• Put together a detailed, unambiguous policy dealing with what business matters your direct reports are permitted to post on public sites. Make clear there are NO exceptions.

And deliver the rules in the form of a feedback discussion.

# TECHNOFEEDBACK TOMORROW

I spent more time talking about Facebook in this chapter than any other social media platform because, at the moment, Facebook is by far the largest and most pervasive example of the phenomenon, if not the one likeliest to be used for business purposes. The lessons and the points I have made are the same, I believe — as valid for LinkedIn or Twitter as vehicles for business communications as for Facebook.

But if I had been writing this chapter just a few years ago, the example I used would have been MySpace (remember that?).

The real point is not only that technology changes almost everything, and changes it *fast*, but that technology itself is in a constant state of flux. No one knows what tomorrow's hot communications platform or device will be — but there will be fortunes won (and lost) in search of it.

You may, for instance, be part of a company that has deployed an organization-wide human resource (and other purposes) system such as Workday, PeopleSoft from Oracle, SAP, or another. In such cases, you will likely be provided with pre-existing templates for personnel reviews, employee evaluations, etc.

Obviously, your formal reviews and assessments will be integrated into the company's system and placed in the format that the system provides. But effective feedback, as I've shown, is far more than a periodic formal review or assessment. You will find that the lessons and techniques presented in this book integrate easily, efficiently, and effectively with any performance management review system or human resource software you may encounter.

In terms of the role of technology in communicating effective feedback, this makes an even larger point.

Whatever the technology platform you're using to deliver feedback, the core values that define effective feedback remain the same. *The medium is the message,* Marshall McLuhan said, and he playfully reminded us that the medium is also the *massage,* the *mass age,* and the *mess age,* and even gave the title *The Medium is the Massage* to one of his books. The medium you use will affect the way you craft and communicate your feedback, but the core purpose and goal of the feedback remains the same:

> Feedback is information that is shared with another person for the distinct purpose of improving results or relationships. Effective feedback is not venting, shaming, or giving in to excuses.

And that goes for *whatever* the next technological revolution, or the one after that, brings.

# TIPS, TOOLS, & TACTICS

TIP: If possible, respond in kind to electronic messages — a txt to you should receive a txt in return (if it requires any reply at all), an email an email, and so on. (And by the way, I feel the same way about wine; Italian wine with the foods of Italy, French with the French, California wine with American food, and so forth.)
  • When your reply to a text would require more space than a txt permits, for instance, say so in a txt:
    ✧  *Ths needs mre discussion — call me @ 2pm*

TIP: Use appropriate language, salutation, and other conventions for various technologies:
  • Abbreviations acceptable in a txt are not acceptable in an email, for instance.
  • Review the rules with all direct reports and team members.

TIP: When a direct report comes up with an especially effective approach to using technology in the course of work, share the approach with the rest of the team. Discuss and analyze what makes it effective, and look for ways to adapt the approach to other purposes — and possibly other technologies.

TOOL: Consider designing an email form for your direct reports (and other members of your team), essentially an electronic letterhead that identifies your direct reports as part of your group — this may require checking with your overall company policy, and, if approved, having the form designed.

TOOL: If the members of your team use their own technology — BYOD (Bring Your Own Device) is catching on at many companies — make sure that all communications between your device (including software) and theirs can be opened and read.

TOOL: Paper still has a place — an important one! Put to use the definite advantages of paper media, including:
- Stationery
- Greeting cards
- Post cards
- Printed newsletters (but only if they've got something to say!)

TACTIC: Instruct your direct reports never to send internal emails from unsecured public Internet access points and hotspots.

TACTIC: Standardize security measures and procedures among your direct reports, ensuring that all are up-to-date on virus protection, frequency of changing passwords, and understanding how to avoid exposing themselves — and your feedback — to unwanted intrusions.

TACTIC: Put together a team-wide newsletter (whether on paper or electronically) focused on general feedback about your business. Invite — or demand, if necessary — regular participation from all members.

**TACTIC:** Find out who among your direct reports is most tech-savvy, then use her or him as resource for *all* members of your team.

*People who ask confidently get more than those who are hesitant and uncertain. When you've figured out what you want to ask for, do it with certainty, boldness, and confidence.*

Jack Canfield, creator of the *Chicken Soup for the Soul* franchise

*"How am I doing?"*

*Ed Koch, running for Mayor of New York*

# CHAPTER EIGHT

# HOW'M I DOING?

# THE ART OF *RECEIVING* FEEDBACK

Remember the late Ed Koch, New York City's irrepressibly popular and equally irrepressibly unpopular mayor?

If you do, you undoubtedly remember Koch's exuberantly shouted catchphrase:

*HOW'M I DOING?*

Everywhere Koch went, and to everyone he encountered, he would pose that simple, profound question.

And in doing so, Koch was not only seeking feedback — ask that open a question of any New Yorker, and you'd better be prepared for feedback! — he was also sending a strong signal that feedback was the heartblood of his administration.

More than that, he was making clear that in his mayoralty, feedback flowed both ways.

In fact, to be effective, feedback *must* flow both ways.

If you're not actively seeking feedback from your line reports — and making clear that you *welcome* their feedback — you're not creating a Feedback Culture.

*But,* by actively making clear not only that feedback *can flow* both ways, but also that you *expect* it to, you're taking a large step toward establishing a Feedback Culture.

Crucially, you are *setting a feedback example.*

More than that, by asking — in your *own* way — "How'm I doing?" you're:

- Establishing yourself as someone who understand the importance of feedback
- Making clear that you *value* feedback
- Giving permission for others to *provide* feedback
- Showing that you can "take" honest feedback
- Demonstrating to employees that feedback isn't anything to be "afraid of"
- Accelerating, by example, the flow of feedback through your organization

That may seem like a lot to accomplish with three small words.

But as I said a moment ago, "How'm I doing?" is a profound question — when it's asked by someone in a position of authority.

It's also a profound question when asked by a direct report — and one that requires immediate, specific response. (When your direct reports are consistently asking "How'm I doing?" — and are asking it in full awareness that your response will be absolutely candid — you'll know that you've taken a step toward creating a viable Feedback Culture.)

There's one other benefit that comes from making public — or at least open — requests for feedback:

- You establish yourself as your organization's "feedback evangelist" — someone who understands effective feedback and puts it to work, showing people its effectiveness, not just telling them about it.

Try it! You may be surprised at just how powerful— and contagious! — a model Ed Koch can be.

# FEEDBACK FEEDS BACK!

Here's one of the oldest sayings around, a phrase we've all heard and used since childhood:

*You can dish it out — but you can't take it in.*

Simple, to-the-point, accurate about most of us, at least some of the time — and a description that's virtually the exact opposite of a far newer and more appealing phrase, one that's embodied in the name of our training program:

*I LOVE FEEDBACK!*

We've covered the art of giving good feedback pretty extensively. You know how to "dish it out" — though, clearly, that's not a phrase that applies to effective feedback graciously presented.

It's time to focus on the other side of the coin: how to receive feedback. Knowing how to be a gracious recipient is just as important to your team's success as knowing how to be an effective communicator.

Maybe even more so.

Your ability not only to accept and evaluate feedback from your direct reports (and, of course, from those you answer to) but also to welcome and, indeed, *invite* honest feedback is every bit as important as your ability to provide effective feedback..

Here are some quick questions to ask yourself:

- Are you *consistently* letting your direct reports (or your students or your own kids, for that matter) talk to you candidly?
- Do you create an atmosphere conducive to others giving you feedback?
- Do you handle yourself well when you get feedback?
- Are you hearing feedback about your performance through the grapevine, or are you getting feedback directly?
- How often do you *ask* for feedback?

Keep your quick answers in mind when you take this quiz to find out, in more detail, where you stand when it comes to receiving feedback:

# Self Assessment on SEEKING and RECEIVING Feedback

**Answer the questions by circling the number that represents the best response. Then total your results.**

| | STRONGLY DISAGREE | | | | STRONGLY AGREE |
|---|---|---|---|---|---|
| 1. I encourage my supervisor (and employees/colleagues) to give me honest feedback about my work. | 1 | 2 | 3 | 4 | 5 |
| 2. I generally have an attitude of openness and interest when receiving feedback on my performance. | 1 | 2 | 3 | 4 | 5 |
| 3. I solicit feedback from my supervisor/others to help me acheive my goals in my development plan. | 1 | 2 | 3 | 4 | 5 |
| 4. I use quarterly performance reviews to ask for feedback from my supervisor. | 1 | 2 | 3 | 4 | 5 |
| 5. I regularly seek out my supervisor's informal input about my performance at work. | 1 | 2 | 3 | 4 | 5 |
| 6. People would say I attentively and respectfully listen to them when discussing work issues. | 1 | 2 | 3 | 4 | 5 |
| 7. I feel comfortable bringing up tough issues for discussion with my supervisor. | 1 | 2 | 3 | 4 | 5 |
| 8. When I receive feedback I don't agree with. I am able to deal with it effectively. | 1 | 2 | 3 | 4 | 5 |
| 9. I'm able to productively manage my emotions when having difficult conversations. | 1 | 2 | 3 | 4 | 5 |
| 10. I love feedback. | 1 | 2 | 3 | 4 | 5 |
| | | | | | TOTAL SCORE |

**RESULTS:**

10-30  Red Alert! Re-invent your approach to seeking and receiving feedback.
31-37  Strongly mediocre feedback skills
38-40  Good feedback abilities, with exciting opportunities to improve
45-50  Olympic level feedback skills

How'd you do? If you're not pleased with your score, don't worry. For a lot of us, probably for *most* of us, receiving feedback is as difficult as giving it.

In this chapter, I'm going to show you how to get comfortable with hearing others critique you. I'll teach you how to get your direct reports to give you honest feedback. And I'll help you get into the zone so that you'll want to receive honest feedback, and you'll welcome it as a valuable tool to help you improve your performance and the company's bottom line.

And, not at all coincidentally, you'll take a large step toward creating a true Feedback Culture.

## YOU CAN'T GET AN ANSWER IF YOU DON'T ASK A QUESTION

As with every other aspect of the **iLoveFeedback** program, there are specific strategies for receiving feedback. First among them:

*ASK FOR IT*

Sounds disarmingly simple, doesn't it?

But this is one area where way too many people fail. We're so busy preparing and delivering feedback, dishing out compliments and criticism, or avoiding it altogether, that we forget to turn around and ask for some in return, particularly from our direct reports.

Yet the more you ask, the better you'll understand how your manager feels about your work, or how your direct reports see you, how they think you're doing, and whether or not your management style is working for them. (If you are a direct report, this goes for you as well for asking your colleagues or your boss or partner.) Nervous about asking? Perhaps even *afraid* to ask? Relax — you're not alone.

If you're a manger or supervisor, you should know that your direct reports can see what mistakes you're making, what areas could be improved, but *they* might be afraid to bring up the subject. It's up to you to dissolve their fears by asking for feedback and letting them know that you're not going to punish them for whatever they tell you.

If you're asking for feedback from your manager or a colleague, your request will be seen as a signal of your enthusiasm, diligence, and understanding of the importance of continually seeking to improve your performance. Think of Ed Koch — he was the mayor — but he also knew who he *really* worked for, and constantly addressed his question to every New Yorker he encountered.

So pick your moment — after putting on your own oxygen mask and finding your Feedback Zone — and take a breath. Then pose a simple question to one of your direct reports:

*"How'm I doing?"*

Actually, you'll want the question to be brief but specific — like all good feedback — and address an aspect of your management relationship with the direct report:

*"What's your assessment of the information and direction you receive from me — and the manner in which I deliver it?"*

That's too wordy, of course, but a good starting point that can be refined and sharpened before you ask the question. And once you do muster the guts to ask for feedback, don't be surprised to find yourself rewarded with insights and epiphanies that'll help you do your job more effectively.

Some of the comments may sting — make clear that you don't take the comments personally, any more than your feedback to them is intended as personal commentary. Your ability to accept legitimate feedback both gracefully and graciously is another key building block in the creation of a Feedback Culture.

Your willingness to invite feedback is not a sign of weakness. It's an act of strength. But it must be presented as one. Your question must be asked confidently, and in a relaxed, professional manner.

In the early stages, you might have to ask often until they finally trust you and realize you're serious about getting feedback.

## DO YOU KNOW HOW THEY WANT TO TALK TO YOU?

In much the same way that you design your feedback sessions to suit the preferences, personality, and thinking styles of your direct reports, be alert for the same qualities and preferences when they are the ones providing the feedback:

- How do your team members want to give you feedback?
- Would they prefer a group setting for preliminary feedback goal-setting sessions, or would each person prefer that you lay the groundwork for the feedback culture individually in a private setting?
- Are they comfortable putting their comments in writing -- with the understanding that their written comments will be explored in face-to-face conversations?

Their preferences should match your assessment of them. The more assertive, expressive individuals will be fine talking to you, but the less assertive and expressive ones are going to want to do it through a memo or an email.

The same is true if you are seeking feedback from a superior: Send the request in the format and medium that the superior is most comfortable with.

Remember Chapter Four's discussion of the Emergenetics Profile. Use this to better understand your direct reports' individual preferences. When you better understand yourself and those with whom you exchange feedback, you're in a better position to maximize feedback style and value.

Based on your understanding of your direct reports, you may decide that directly asking the initial question is too large an initial step. The solution is simple — *start smaller!*

If you and your direct reports are in the same building, you might even consider putting a box in the hallway and inviting everyone to leave you feedback anonymously. The problem with this approach is that you won't be able to address specific concerns with the individual who brought the issue up. But that's not precisely the point or the function of the feedback box.

The purpose is to introduce the idea of feedback flowing upstream as well as down. Once your people get comfortable with giving you feedback, get rid of the box and invite them to approach you directly.

Establishing an initial feedback box can be a little trickier when you and your direct reports don't share the same workspace, but

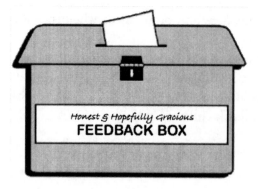

Honest & Hopefully Gracious
**FEEDBACK BOX**

you can experiment with having direct reports create separate email accounts, anonymous ones, that can be used to start the feedback ball rolling.

Whatever approach, if any, you take to anonymous feedback, bear in mind that it's only a preliminary step. As soon as possible, bring the feedback out into the open, where it belongs.

# "GET" IT — BUT DON'T LET IT GET TO YOU

Earlier I mentioned that some of the feedback you receive might sting. That's unavoidable. What *is* avoidable — and must be avoided — is letting the feedback "get" to you.

I'm reminded of...*beekeepers!* In the initial stages of keeping bees, it's not unusual to be stung, and stung often. As the apiarist (the official word for beekeeper) grows more skilled at working the hives, the number of stings declines. But something else happens —

If you're working with bees, you are going to get stung occasionally, no matter how skilled you are. But over time the effect of the stings diminishes; the apiarist builds up both an immunity and a familiarity with the experience that minimizes the pain and places it in its proper perspective.

My own version of this, acquired over the years is the slogan:
*Take feedback seriously, not personally.*

This is, I will be the first to admit, easier said than done. Human nature, company politics, thinking styles, and behavioral styles are just some of the things that keep us from asking for feedback regularly.

But I will also tell you that it's very much worth doing.

And it's worth doing right — which means you won't be taking the feedback personally.

A manager *can't* take it personally. Feedback, even painfully negative feedback, isn't your loved one telling you, "I'm leaving you." It's not a form of rejection or betrayal or anything else involving strong emotion. Feedback is simply someone at work giving you a crucial piece of information that's intended ultimately to help you do your job better — or at least start a worthwhile dialogue about it.

Think of professional athletes. They don't pout or have a breakdown every time a coach tells them to improve. They listen closely, attentive to the coach's insights into precisely how the improvement can best be achieved. Athletes know that their coach has their best interest in mind. They take his or her advice seriously but not personally. And they do what it takes to improve their performance.

I realize that it takes some learning, some retraining, to get yourself to the point where you can see feedback as constructive criticism and not a personal attack. Those first bee stings do hurt, but the apiarist learns to deal with them in order to care for the hives — and eventually harvest the honey.

Give yourself time. It'll get easier. And the experience will grow easier and more comfortable quicker if you apply basic feedback rules and practices to yourself — *do as you say as well as you do:*

- You'll receive feedback better when you're in your right zone. Don't ask for feedback when you're anxious or angry, when you've got low energy, when you're stressed out or feeling burned out.
- Get yourself into your high-performance zone first.
- Get yourself into a state where you're energized, confident, calm, focused, flexible, and open to having fun.
- First ask yourself, "How am I feeling?" When you're at the top of your game, you're ready to ask others, "How am I doing?"

In other words: Put on your own oxygen mask first when seeking feedback for yourself as well as providing it for others.

# INTERLUDE

## WHY DID ABRAHAM LINCOLN GROW A BEARD?

Honest Abe's beard, one of his most familiar features, came about as a result of feedback...in this case, feedback in the form of a letter from an 11-year-old girl who had seen him speak. Unlike most adults (including his political advisors), she possessed the innocence and candor to tell him what she thought about his appearance.

*Abraham Lincoln*

In Doris Kearns Godwin's book on Lincoln, *Team of Rivals*, she talks of Lincoln as he gets ready for his first term as president. He is answering some of the many letters he received when he came across one from a young girl. Kearns writes the following:

"In mid-October, he replied to eleven-year-old Grace Bedell, who had recommended that he grow a beard, 'for your face is so thin,' and 'all the ladies like whiskers.'...He answered, 'As to the whiskers, having never worn any, do you not think people would call it a piece of silly affection if I were to begin it now?'

"Nonetheless, he proceeded to grow a beard. By January 1861, John Hay [his chief of staff] would pen a witty couplet: 'Election news Abe's hirsute fancy warrant — Apparent hair becomes heir apparent.'"

One could almost see Lincoln looking in the mirror and thinking to himself, "Maybe I would look better with a beard; I think I'll give it a try." This is a true yet fanciful story, but his ability to listen to feedback, and to purposefully seek it out, is shown in yet another scene from Goodwin's book.

Toward the end of the Civil War, rumors had begun to float that Lincoln had received and refused peace offerings from the Confederates. To answer the rumors, Lincoln wrote a letter to be read aloud at a mass rally in Chicago.

Godwin writes: "After completing an early draft, Lincoln searched out someone to listen as he read it aloud...Entering the [White House] library, the president was delighted to find William Stoddard. 'Ah! I'm glad you're here, come over into my room. What I want is an audience. Nothing sounds the same when there isn't anyone to hear it and find fault with it.'"

Seeking out feedback was a habit for Abraham Lincoln, and the feedback sessions (as you can see in Spielberg's great film *Lincoln*) were robust and candid.

HOW'M I DOING?

ED KOCH, former three-term mayor of New York City, when he was running for his first term was not doing well until he started asking New Yorkers "How'm I doing?" — which seemed to turn the tide to his side.

The idea of a potential political leader throwing his arms out at every meeting and speech resonated because it somehow made him vulnerable perhaps, but more so because it gave the perception that he was curious (which he was) and open to their ideas. The phrase became his brand, and he became an NYC icon.

*Ed Koch*

"How'm I doing?" was a part of most newspaper articles and many news broadcasts covering his funeral. "No mayor, I think, has ever embodied the spirit of New York City like he did," Mayor Michael Bloomberg told the mourners, "and I don't think anyone ever will. Tough and loud, brash and irreverent, full of humor and chutzpah — he was our city's quintessential mayor."

He, like Lincoln, was also known to give feedback as well as receive it. At the funeral, former president Bill Clinton held up a bunch of letters he had received from Koch giving both solicited and unsolicited feedback on Clinton's policies.

What would happen in your company (or household) if everyone were encouraged to ask frequently, "How'm I doing?"

# LEARN HOW TO LISTEN

If you're serious about having others give you feedback, you've got to make that seriousness clear to them.

You do this by being an attentive listener.

Think about it. The person whose feedback you've requested has probably been sweating about it all morning. He's been rehearsing what to tell you in his mind over and over again. He's mustered the courage to walk into your office and give you honest, right-between-the-eyes feedback. The least you can do is honor that courage, that chutzpah, by giving him your undivided attention.

After all — and, actually, *above* all — *you asked for it!*

When somebody wants to talk to you, whether or not you've requested the feedback, make the time to listen, and make yourself *ready* to listen:

- Schedule an appropriate time and place for the conversation.
- Give the person enough time to talk.
- Recognize that this isn't necessarily easy for her or him. Don't make it any harder on them by appearing distracted or disinterested.
- When they're done, whatever they've said to you, be sure to express thanks for the feedback discussion. This opens the door to future sessions — which is what you want.

Practice effective listening skills, and put them on display for your nervous direct report:

- Stay attentive to the emotional cues of the speaker, being attentive to context as well as content.
- Practice good, nonverbal listening, especially by making eye contact and maintaining an open (not closed) posture. (Have all calls held until the meeting is over, for instance.)
- Give the speaker your undivided attention.
- Ask questions, not defensively but to make sure you have it right. The psychological term for this is "active listening" — e.g., "What I hear you saying is that I'm too abrupt; is that right?"
- Try to empathize, taking the other person's perspective.

It will be far easier for your direct reports to give you the feedback you need if they know that you're actually going to listen to them.

# STEER CLEAR OF CONVERSATIONAL PITFALLS

What's a conversational pitfall?

Anything that brings open, productive, constructive conversation to an abrupt halt.

Defensiveness is a prime example of a pitfall.

We understand the importance of getting into the zone before receiving feedback. Having your own oxygen mask in place, and being comfortably ensconced in your Feedback Zone, keeps you from becoming defensive, angry, or resentful toward the person offering you feedback. You don't want to get dragged down by these energy-depleting emotions. And you don't want to make the other person angry, resentful, or defensive toward you.

Another conversation pitfall is apathy. You've got to care about what the other person's telling you. If you're distracted, or you're just going through the motions without really caring about what they're telling you, they're going to see right through you. You risk having your direct reports essentially give up, throwing their hands in the air and asking themselves, *What's the point?* Avoid the apathy pitfall. Remain attentive and engaged.

Let the other person speak. Don't interrupt or try to finish his sentences for him. Let him talk. You're not in a position to be making assumptions. You're at a receptive place, a 100% listener.

I think one of the major things we need to learn is how to:

*Become friends with silence.*

One of the greatest benefits of silence is that it allows you to think. Feedback sessions are not about nonstop talking. Allow those moments of silence in. It may be that the person giving you feedback needs a moment or two to collect her thoughts. Grant her that time, without fidgeting or looking at the clock.

Silence works for you as well. During a pause you will have time to:

- Process the feedback and related information you've just received.
- Plan your response.
- Always remember, though, that your processing and planning time comes during the silences, not during the conversation.

- When the feedback recipient is speaking, your number-one responsibility is to pay attention — the worst thing you can do is fail to listen when your direct report or subordinate is speaking.

You'll not have the time — you'll want it. You certainly don't want to be planning what to say while the other person is talking — that's a distraction, and it's another one of those conversation pitfalls.

But bear in mind that your silence can all too easily be misinterpreted:

- What's he thinking?
- What was *I* thinking — should have kept my mouth shut!
- What did I say wrong?
- Why isn't he *talking* to me?

At the onset of your feedback session, offer these words: "If you say something, and afterward I'm silent for a minute, it's because I'm thinking about it. I don't want to be preparing my answer while you're talking. Therefore, once I've heard you, it's going to take me a minute or two to think about what to say back to you."

## WHEN BAD FEEDBACK HAPPENS TO GOOD PEOPLE

You're human.

You're not going to agree with every piece of feedback you receive. And frankly, some of it is going to be off-base and completely unfair. So, what do you do?

First, keep yourself calm.

- Avoid those most common pitfalls: anger, defensiveness, resentment.
- Stay in your peak Feedback Zone.
- Stay calm — I can't emphasize this one enough.
- Take a few deep breaths to calm down.

Remember —

*Take it seriously, not personally.*

And show that you take it seriously — even if it's way off-base: Handle it by engaging in a dialogue about the feedback.

One of the best keys to handling feedback you don't agree with is to ask questions.

It's perfectly OK for you to ask questions about everything the person says to you. Try phrases like these:

- Now, tell me again what you're saying.
- Would you repeat that in a different way so I really get it? I want to fully understand what you're conveying here.
- How would you tell someone else about this feedback you're giving me — what would someone else hear you saying?

Asking questions works a lot like silence. It slows people down. If this person comes in ready to rip you, and you start asking questions, then you slow her or him down; you slow down the thinking process. And in turn, you change the energy level, often diffusing whatever anger or negativity the other person brought in.

Slowing the process down through questions is a wonderful way to maintain calmness. That's another key to handling feedback you don't like.

It's an act of courage to ask questions when somebody tells you something you're not prepared to hear. It might be tough to do, but it truly works in your favor. When you choose to actively participate in this dialogue process, it puts you in a better place emotionally. So go ahead, ask questions. Ask for clarification. Make sure you understand the feedback you've just been given.

By doing so, you're not only improving the feedback session — and perhaps turning it around completely — you're also setting an example...and further nurturing the Feedback Culture.

## TIPS, TOOLS, & TACTICS

TIP: *Ask for feedback* — invite input from your direct reports about *your* performance. *"How'm I doing?"* is a profound and effective question. Call a spouse, partner, your kids, a neighbor, anybody — and practice asking for feedback.

TIP: Stay in your peak Feedback Zone when *receiving* feedback as well as when giving it.

TIP: Take it seriously — not personally.

TOOL: Keep a feedback log on *yourself* — the same sorts of evaluation and commentary that you would record for a direct report:
- Who offered the feedback?
- What was the specific feedback?
- How did you receive the feedback?
- What follow-up is needed?

TOOL: Consider setting up a small review card where you'll note the feedback you received — and which of your direct reports provided it. Such a tool can be invaluable as you assess the direct report's feedback skills, or lack of them. Notations on this card reveal an entirely different aspect of the direct report's relationship to feedback — and to you.

TOOL: Give the feedback quiz from the opening pages of the book to your team, but remind them afterward that, "We're all going to get better at this." Then, over the following week, pick three items that need improvement, and focus on raising the team members' capabilities and comfort level with those areas.

TACTIC: Ask questions and seek clarification when receiving negative feedback.

TACTIC: Make friends with silence — you don't have to fill every second of a meeting with talk. And you shouldn't. Silence gives you time to think, plan — and prepare better feedback.

TACTIC: If a direct report is hesitant to offer candid feedback, shift the focus to the direct report: "I want you to help me help you. How can I do that best? What am I doing right and what could I improve upon in our communications?"

*We go through life
at 100 miles per hour
with our eyes firmly fixed
on the rear view mirror...*

Marshall McLuhan

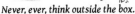

*Never, ever, think outside the box.*

# CHAPTER NINE

# GETTING CREATIVE
# WITH FEEDBACK

**W**hat does *creativity have to do with feedback?*
 That's a question I've heard countless times — and to which my response is constant and enthusiastic:
*A LOT!*
Here's a comment I've heard almost as often:
 *But I'm not creative!*
My equally constant and equally enthusiastic response is:
 *SURE YOU ARE!*
The problem — if you doubt your creativity — could be a misunderstanding of what I mean by creativity. Fortunately, that misunderstanding may not be as extreme - or as messy! -- as the cat in the cartoon at the head of this chapter and, like the cat, it's something that can be corrected.

I'm not talking about the sort of creativity that the movies depict by having a character put on a beret and move to Paris or Greenwich Village. And even less am I talking about the sort of anguished, agonizing creativity that shows up in melodramas about great painters or musicians.

Before we go further, let's talk about what creativity really means and why you might think you don't possess it (or that it's not a natural part of your thinking style).

The word *creativity* is from the Latin creo, to make or to create. The Greeks didn't have a word for "to create"; they used "to discover." Man didn't create: It was only through the Muses that the gods helped man discover or uncover new things or ideas.

Not until the Renaissance drifted into the Enlightenment did we begin to think that man, not just God, could create.

Today, creativity belongs to everybody.

Including you...if you want it.

---

### HOW DO *YOU* DEFINE CREATIVITY?
### IT COULD DEPEND ON YOUR THINKING STYLE

When I speak of creativity, I am not talking of the sort that produces great works of art (although if you possess that sort of gift I envy you).

Rather, I am talking about the ability to bring a variety of insights, thoughts, experiences, and ideas to your feedback and, in a larger sense, to your work.

Approached with this definition in mind, *creativity* becomes something we all possess, and can all develop and apply to our lives and work.

Think of the four quadrants we explored in our discussion of Emergenetics (Analytical, Structural, Social, and Conceptual), and remember that creativity manifests itself differently in each of us. Imagine, for instance, the difference in feedback sessions you would get from Robin Williams and General George S. Patton or Steve Jobs and Martha Stewart.

The feedback might be fundamentally the same in terms of content but vastly different in terms of context. Creativity is similar.

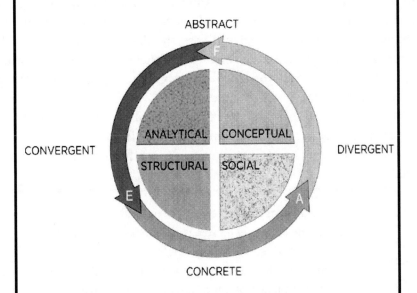

Think of the art of scheduling: To a Structural thinker, logistics can be as creative as painting or composing, as UPS has shown in its ads about how creative the company's approach to logistics is.

If you've ever been to a Disney theme park, you'll immediately understand what I'm talking about: At Disney parks, the queues of families waiting to board a ride or enter an attraction are guided through pleasantly arranged pathways that make even long lines not just bearable but actually fun. They are an excellent example of a combination of Structural thinking and Social thinking creativity. Your own dominant thinking style will help determine — but not dictate — the forms and types of creativity you bring to your feedback.

To put it in basic terms, the sort of creativity that I'm talking about is the opposite of "taking it for granted" or "doing the minimum required." You wouldn't be reading this book if either of those phrases applied to your approach to life and work.

The creativity I'm taking about in this chapter is the extra thought, reflection, and insight that you can bring to your work, your family and personal life, your hobbies and avocations. The touch of humor, the addition of appropriate playfulness, the change of scenery, the different approach to ideas, the small extra touches that lift the routine at least part of the way toward the memorable and, when everything clicks just right, the unforgettable.

They are all ways of enhancing feedback and at the same time tools for getting ourselves and our teams "unstuck" from routine.

Now we're going to look at ways to bring that creativity to your feedback.

> To be creative, one must be flexible, not rigid.
>
> You must be able to explore a wide variety of options for any problem. The search for the single answer will stick us every time. You should strive for a Zen-like ability to appreciate the absurdity of any situation and jump in anyway with as much zest and joy as possible.
>
> From *CATCHFIRE* by Peter McLaughlin

Think about the various elements of feedback we explored in the earlier chapters.

Putting them all together, you should not be surprised that in some important ways, most effective feedback is creative — at least all feedback that follows a successfully implemented Feedback Revolution.

As I've shown throughout the pages of this book — and as is demonstrated with hands-on examples in the iLoveFeedback program — effective feedback draws upon:

- Realism
- Specificity
- Timeliness
- Consideration
- Empathy
- Context

Those final two points are crucial when you are bringing creativity to the feedback session. Be sure you understand what your team is facing — and sensing — before you "send in the clowns," as the Stephen Sondheim song goes. In short, if you're delivering tough feedback. It's probably not the right time for balloons.

All of these points I've made so far are really just another way of saying that

*THERE IS NO SUCH THING AS EFFECTIVE PRO FORMA FEEDBACK.*

*EFFECTIVE FEEDBACK ALWAYS REQUIRES SPECIFIC, EMPATHETIC THOUGHT.*

When you apply *thought* with *empathy* to the evaluation, interpretation, analysis, and critique that are the content of the feedback you will be offering, you are also bringing *creativity* to the mix, whether or not you consciously think of it. This is true no matter how rigorously or relentlessly logical you seek to be in the preparation of the feedback message.

Your brain is making connections as you assemble and review the relevant information, and your mind is fashioning those connections into patterns and presentations that tailor your message to the recipient, the current business need, the medium by which the feedback will be conveyed or delivered.

Those connections — the unique qualities of your mind that you bring to and combine with the specific message you are crafting — are absolutely an example of creativity at work.

So accept the fact — you're creative!

More than that, *embrace the fact:* YOU'RE CREATIVE!

And so, in their own way, are all the people to whom you'll be providing feedback — and from whom you'll be receiving it.

Now that we've established that at even its most basic level, effective feedback can be a creative process, let's take a look at how even a little thought can raise that creativity — and the effectiveness of the feedback — to the next level and beyond.

In the course of this chapter we'll examine ways in which creativity can enhance virtually every feedback situation, but let's start by revisiting the most structured of such situations — the formal annual performance review.

## MATTERS OF FORM:
## PERFORMANCE MANAGEMENT PROGRAMS

I pointed out just now that *EFFECTIVE FEEDBACK IS NEVER ROUTINE OR PRO FORMA.*

This is true no matter how rigorously your company adheres to a review template or formal Performance Management System.

Ineffective managers can all too easily succumb to the temptation to bring a "routine" approach to such systems and the forms, checklists, and "grades" that companies use in their implementation.

See if something like this doesn't strike a familiar note, perhaps reminding you of ineffective managers from your own past (or even your present!):

- Fill out the forms.
- Check the boxes.
- Assign the grade or evaluation score.
- Show the forms to the recipient — and get the process over with as quickly as possible.
- Turn the signed forms in to the appropriate department.
- Repeat the process once a year.

If you've ever experienced such a bored or lackadaisical approach to an annual review, you know first-hand just how frustrating — or actually depressing — such an experience can be.

Think about the messages such an approach sends. Another full year of work and effort has passed, and as a reward the direct report receives:

- A bored or hasty (and often both!) recitation of required check-off points
- A catalog, rarely elaborated on or examined in detail, of areas for improvement
- An equally routine check-off of areas of "satisfactory" performance

- A generally uninspiring and unelaborated set of "goals" for the following year
- An announcement of an increase in compensation, if appropriate

(That final element, needless to say, is likely to be the *only* thing the direct report really remembers from the review.)

> A survey conducted by the Society for Human Resources Management concluded that more than 90 per cent of performance appraisal systems fail, with both managers and employees saying that they dread the execution of this process. As a matter of fact, it is common practice for HR departments to routinely report that they have a desperately hard time getting managers to deal with the personal appraisals of their subordinates.
>
> *Malta Independent,* May 21, 2013

Is it any wonder that most managers — and most direct reports — dread the approach of Review Season?

In the course of working with numerous corporations and organizations seeking to identify the "elephant in the room," I've heard horror stories about this dreaded exercise; its manifestation in dull, boring, low-value reviews and assessments; and its effect on morale and motivation.

And, frankly, I've experienced it personally.

In my case, the lack of thoughtful, forward-looking, *creative* feedback led me to look for other challenges...at other employers.

This is NOT the intent of even the most the rigorously structured Performance Management System — or the company that uses it.

Rather, those systems exist to provide a manageable and efficient framework for sorting and processing the information contained in your evaluation of your team members, as well as to provide you with a convenient structure for reminding yourself of the matters that must be covered in an annual review.

Taking that structure, combining it with your understanding of the elements of effective feedback, adding your own creativity, you can transform the dreaded review into a welcome, worthwhile, and truly memorable experience.

# INTERLUDE

## TOM PETERS AND JAY LENO —
## EFFECTIVE FEEDBACK SATISFIES YOURSELF

Tom Peters preaches getting feedback, especially from clients. As he says in his new book, *The Little Big Things*: "I crave great 'customer feedback' — but in no way, shape, or form am I trying to 'satisfy my customer.'"

"I am, I repeat, trying instead to satisfy *me*, my own deep neediness to reach out and grab my customer and connect with my customer over ideas that consume and devour me."

*Tom Peters*

Tom Peters, one of the foremost commentators, authors *(In Search of Excellence)*, and speakers on business (and life) today, not only loves feedback, but he uses it in very creative ways. He listens to feedback, gets it, and turns it into new and innovative ways to come back at his clients with outrageous ideas to consider.

Here's some creative feedback to managers and parents about change and creativity: "The power to invent (and execute) is switching/flipping rapidly/inexorably to the network. 'Me' is transitioning to 'we' — as consumers and producers." If consumers are part of your team, as opposed to the outsiders we perform for, how would that change all of your feedback systems?

I even love Peters' word choice as a bolster to getting more creative at giving feedback. Words like: astonishing, entrancing, revolutionary, staggering, amazing.

Try putting a few of those words in your prep work for feedback... creativity will flow.

In this decade-old picture of Jay Leno and me resides a story of his ability to give candid yet positive and creative feedback.

I was introduced to Jay by a colleague, who happened to be a long-time friend of Jay. He pitched me for a spot on the *Tonight Show* as a new author of a potentially best-selling book.

Jay did not miss a beat and answered with candor and humor that "businesspeople and authors are too boring" to be on his show.

"But because you are a seemingly good fellow, I will have our photographer snap a picture of us." He actually had me on stage in the guest chair while we talked and laughed.

Jay's sense of humor and generosity very much impressed me (he doesn't seem to change from the talk show host role to real life). The fact that I was turned down in a straightforward yet creative and fun way became a source of pride.

As I was writing this book, the inci-

*Peter McLaughlin and Jay Leno*

dent popped back into my head, with a new awareness that Jay Leno had built a habit of creative feedback. Instead of falling back on "I'll have my producer get back to you," and then never doing it, he handled it on the spot with candor, creativity, and fun.

"How do you get to Carnegie Hall?" the violinist asked the cabbie. "With a lot of practice," he answered.

How do you learn to give straightforward and even creative feedback so people will accept it with a smile? You guessed it...Practice.

# CREATING A FEEDBACK EXPERIENCE

Ask yourself:
- **WHY?** *To improve performance and ensure understanding of both expectations and possibilities.*
- **WHERE** will my direct reports receive their review?
- **WHEN** (time of day) will the review take place?
- **HOW** will the review be presented?
- **WHAT** will the direct report take away from the review?

Each of these questions is an opportunity for a touch of creativity:
- **WHY:** Not simply to fulfill an annual (or more frequent) company requirement (although that's important), but also to renew and reinvigorate — or establish, with new members of your team — a feedback-rich conversation between you and the team member.
- **WHERE:** If practical, conduct the reviews in a new or unexpected — though appropriate — setting; or consider some temporary design amendments or adjustments to your office or meeting space in order to signal that this is a new and out-of-the-ordinary experience.
- **WHEN:** Pick a time of day when energy levels are high, concentration is sharp; don't schedule review for end-of-day or at the last possible time in the review season.
- **HOW:** Consider (again, if appropriate) a "formal" invitation along the lines of: *Let's schedule a conversation to review the past year and look especially closely at the ups and downs of our work, with an eye toward making next year even more rewarding.*

It can be a little more challenging to add a touch of creativity to feedback intended to flow upstream: Be certain that you understand your manager or supervisor's attitude toward creative "extras" before adding them to your feedback.

Better still, get a sense of your boss's own creativity (or lack of) and how it's expressed (it's there — you may have to look for it, but it *is* there) and tailor your feedback accordingly. But not slavishly: You're appealing to your manager, not imitating her or him.

Obviously, you will take your own approach to these and other matters aimed at elevating the formal review into an *experience* rather than an obligation, and doing so while attending to every required or mandatory element of the Performance Management System.

Of course, this creative approach to the once-a-year review is vastly enhanced — and made vastly easier — if you bring your creativity to *all* of the feedback you deliver during the months leading up to the formal session.

So: Just how do you go about adding a bit of creativity to "everyday" feedback?

The same way — though less "formally!"

## FEEDBACK LOG: MARGIE

Feedback to a musician can be the sweetest music to your ears, or a criticism that cuts to the quick.

In a jazz ensemble, feedback is constant — setting up a phrase for another musician to respond to can feel risky — or sweet and light as a feather.

A pianist I work with, Billy Wallace, is a master at providing feedback. Always encouraging and supportive, he finds something to praise while also giving me a tip to enhance a phrase or play a more complicated chord.

The positive nature of his comments encourages me to take risks and be bolder. I know that if I take a vocal risk and it is not perfect, he will praise me for trying and let me know how I might correct it next time. Also, if I really get myself into a train wreck, he will cover and take over — allowing me to recover, find my composure, and settle down.

Sometimes feedback needs to be immediate and direct.

I remember one gig where the drummer was late, agitated, and upset about a lot of things that had happened to him during the previous week. He was wearing his emotions on his sleeve, and the rest of the group was walking on eggshells around him. After the first tune, in which he set a rhythm that was too fast and too loud, I asked him to please play the tempo that I asked for. He stood up in front of the audience and said, "I don't need this..."

I replied, "OK. Take down your set and go home."

He scowled, sat back down, and waited for the next tune to be called.

I called "'Deed I Do," an old standby jazz standard. I wanted to convey my feelings to him through the lyrics, which are:

*Do I love you — oh my, do I? Honey, 'deed I do*

*Do I need you — oh my, do I? Honey, 'deed I do!*

I sang the entire song directly to him with my back to the audience members (who were pretty confused by this time). At the end of the song, he stood up and held his arms open — we embraced; each of us had tears in our eyes.

My feedback was direct and timely — and, I believe, delivered in a very creative fashion.

All of which helped ensure that it was well-received.

I think about this virtually every time I have feedback to deliver — although in most business situations I can't deliver it in song!

Margie
*(who is a jazz singer on her weekends)*

# HUMOR ME

As the cartoons placed at the head of each chapter show, I'm a great believer in the power of humor to set the stage, offer insight, unlock creativity.

While I understand the sentiments behind the old maxim that states:

*HUMOR HAS ITS PLACE*

I think it's just as important to bear in mind something George Bernard Shaw said:

*". . .THE WORLD DOESN'T CEASE TO BE SERIOUS WHEN SOMEONE LAUGHS ANY MORE THAN IT CEASES TO BE FUNNY WHEN SOMEONE DIES."*

Your common sense and understanding of both a stuation's context and the people involved will let you know when humor is and isn't appropriate. That said, a couple of points should be made — and kept in mind.

A critical feedback session — especially a formal review — may not be the right place to bring out your full arsenal of jokes and quips. There are several reasons for this, including:

- The opportunity for misinterpretation:
  - ✧ You understand the anxiety that accompanies reviews — now imagine how you'd feel if the first thing you heard in your review was a string of one-liners.
- Humor is subjective:
  - ✧ If you've ever had a joke "fall flat," this one is self-explanatory.
- Inappropriate tone or content:
  - ✧ I mean not just the obviously inappropriate — and possibly actionable — content such as sexism, ethnic humor, and so on, but also cutting, biting, or sarcastic humor, especially when it's aimed at your company or at business situations.

Does this mean that I'm advocating a humorless, dour, stern work environment?

Far from it! In fact, an entire chapter of my previous book, *Catchfire*, is devoted to examining humor and its place in work. (You can get a free copy of the *Catchfire* e-book if you stop by my Web site, http://www.petermclaughlin.com/, and sign up for my newsletter.)

What I am saying here is that feedback — even for those who have embraced the Feedback Revolution and the iLoveFeedback program

— is a special type and form of communication, targeted and designed to enhance results.

Feedback sessions should always be energetic, lively, provocative — but not necessarily hilarious! Enlightenment means to "lighten up"; it means moving away from the overly serious feedback discussions that too often dominate in corporate cultures.

Because of the Feedback Culture you have created and nurtured, you will know your team members well enough to know what is and isn't appropriate in feedback sessions, and guide yourself accordingly.

---

### WHAT LINCOLN KNEW

Anyone who's seen Stephen Spielberg's film, *Lincoln*, or read Doris Kearns Goodwin's book, *Team of Rivals*, on which the film was based, is aware of Abraham Lincoln's ability to use a quip or humorous anecdote to great effect in even the most tense and consequential of moments.

What Lincoln understood was that humor was a valuable rhetorical tool, offering the opportunity to relax a bit and helping to defuse tense situations. He also understood that it had to be the right type of humor. This is why eulogies rarely involve slapstick, to use an extreme example. But it's also why, when a speaker at a funeral shares an amusing or even outright funny story about the deceased, our laughter is not nervous or shocked, but genuine and shared. We are grateful to have been reminded of something appropriately light during a somber ceremony.

What Lincoln knew, and put to such successful use, can also find a ready and appreciative audience in your feedback sessions. Try it — they'll like it.

— Peter

---

# CREATE YOUR OWN CREATIVITY

All those old myths about creative people having to wait until inspiration strikes to get any creating done are pretty much just that —

myths. Think about it — if most artists, writers, and composers really did sit back and wait for creativity to descend from the Muses, we'd probably have far fewer great paintings, novels, and symphonies.

Professional "creators" understand that when necessary, creativity can be jump-started, no matter how "uncreative" one feels.

You understand that too. In the Tips, Tools, & Tactics section you'll find some specific strategies for jump-starting your creativity, but for now I want to remind you of the point that was made at the beginning of this chapter:

*CREATIVE, IN A FEEDBACK CONTEXT, DOESN'T MEAN "ARTISTIC" — IT MEANS GIVING YOUR FEEDBACK THE EXTRA ATTENTION, CONSIDERATION, AND ENTHUSIASM THAT ITS RECIPIENTS DESERVE.*

# TIPS, TOOLS, & TACTICS

**TIP:** Before every formal feedback session, take a few minutes to consider how you can reframe your feedback...perhaps using a scene from a film or a book.

**TIP:** Invite creativity from your team members by using role-play or simply asking the question: "What are you hoping I won't ask you about?"

**TIP:** Humor can be tricky — or worse — in feedback contexts; think hard before including a joke in a performance review, or use the joke with a colleague and get her response to the way you might use it with your direct report or your boss.

**TOOL:** Keep an eye out for creative opportunities to give feedback to your team.

**TOOL:** Take them to a pre-season sports practice and have them monitor the coaches and players in their use of feedback, both giving and receiving.

**TOOL:** Is there something creative you can do at the start (or end) of your session to get everyone into the emotional place you want them to be?

**TACTIC:** If you're stuck on a feedback project, try unsticking yourself by approaching the problem in reverse:
- What's the ultimate goal of the session?
- How can you shape your feedback to reach that goal — and do so in a creative, memorable, and effective manner?

**TACTIC:** Readjust your own oxygen mask so you are in the emotional space in which you want people to be.

**TACTIC:** Buy two oxygen masks and do a role-play at the start of the feedback exercise.

*Your first and foremost job as a leader is to take charge of your own energy and then to orchestrate the energy of those around you.*

Peter F. Drucker

*Your oil's fine but your blood-sugar level's a little low.*

## CHAPTER TEN

# CREATING A FEEDBACK CULTURE – FROM BLOOD SUGAR TO *FENG SHUI*

**D**o you love feedback yet?

I hope so, but I also know that this isn't an overnight or, as I said earlier, a single-quarter process.

But by this point I think I've presented a pretty good case that whether you're a team leader or a team member, you need to *want* feedback, and you need to create a mindset among your people where *they* want feedback too.

And the best way to measure your progress is during a formal feedback session.

Don't just take my word for it. Give it a try. Ease into it, if you'd prefer to start slowly...I'm confident that once you start experiencing the benefits of presenting and receiving carefully prepared and thoughtfully presented feedback for yourself, you'll wonder how you managed for so long without it.

Take that first step — and before you know it, feedback will be wanted, expected, anticipated, and appreciated by you and your team members.

A good first step is to rethink and redo the way you approach formal feedback sessions.

Take a serious look at your energy and emotional levels, and how you care for them.

## WHAT'S BLOOD SUGAR GOT TO DO WITH IT?

While it would be an exaggeration to say that even the most relaxed and inviting environments can't overcome low energy levels, it's no exaggeration to say that your body's physical energy state dramatically affects your ability to be effective at anything — work, play, conversation, concentration.

We've all experienced one of "those days" — we feel rundown and lethargic but not really sick; our concentration is no good; we may be irritable for no particular reason.

The culprit? In all likelihood, it's low blood sugar.

In a way, this is as clear an example of feedback as you're ever likely to experience. When your blood sugar drops below certain levels, your body sends unmistakable signals in the form of symptoms, including not only those mentioned above, but also, in extreme cases, serious physical problems including double vision and even fainting.

Fortunately, in most cases, your blood sugar level is something you can control — and the problems you are experiencing with it are also of your own making.

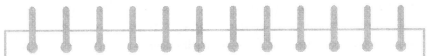

## FEEDBACK LOG: PETER

While I was in graduate school, I also sold real estate. Often I found myself showing homes to out-of-town buyers. They were my favorite clients.

Why? Simple. Out-of-town buyers were often under real-time pressure to buy: Generally one of the spouses had been transferred, or had landed a job in my city. Often they faced the challenges of getting their children enrolled in schools, establishing bank accounts, and all the other responsibilities that accompany establishing residence.

All of this usually meant that there was a good shot at my making a sale before they left town.

The most eye-opening example of the role of low blood sugar happened to me during one of these potential "easy sale" moments. I was showing a young family four or five houses, and I was hopeful to have a deal done by early afternoon. They were all jet-lagged, the kids were arguing, and the parents had very different ideas of style of house and location.

She wanted schools to be close, and sidewalks.

He wanted suburbs and bike trails.

I wanted them out of the car.

By early afternoon, all were in a state of frazzle, and I was trying to be a humorous peacemaker.

Finally at 4 PM, the husband declared that our search was over. He was too exhausted to carry on, the kids were semi-passed out in the

back seat, and she was close to tears. They disembarked at their hotel. She tried to be nice, asking me to call them in the morning. He
marched straight into the hotel without a word. I didn't have the energy to do anything but watch the whole scene in slow motion.

I learned only subsequently that the hidden reality of my failed sales
day was tiredness, brought on partially by blood sugar levels. My plan
should have been to pick them up and get them to breakfast, then arrange the day with stops for water, coffee, or healthy snacks. I needed
a strategy that first and foremost held my own energy levels at a high
positive, and secondly accounted for theirs. I couldn't take control of
the situation with good feedback or any kind of leadership because
my energy was drained.

The results? I lost a relationship; they didn't find a house; and I didn't
even care...

Now think about how your own blood sugar level can affect your nature in a feedback situation, when some minor thing sets you off, or
when during an important moment, you just lost interest; you went
into the tank.

Peter

## THE RIGHT BLOOD SUGAR LEVEL –
## THE FOOD AND MOOD CONNECTION

Prepare for feedback mentally and physically. When you're about to
give or get feedback, be aware that your body chemistry's present con-
dition affects your current mental outlook. Your brain gets nourish-
ment only from glucose and oxygen, so when your blood sugar's too
low, what happens? Your brain goes into panic mode, and your body
follows suit. You're at a precarious point, too easily pushed into the anger and anxiety zone. You're in no "mood" to give or receive feedback.

The food you consume alters your body and brain chemistry. When your blood sugar level spikes and dips as a result of eating overly processed junk foods (such as pastries, chips, and sodas) while starving yourself between meals, it's a sure recipe for fatigue, irritability, and mood swings.

Fruit is a fantastic way to remedy the situation. I've given this advice over and over again at countless companies: Get rid of your greasy, sugary doughnuts and replace them with fresh fruit. What a difference this makes in company meetings. Creativity goes up, and more gets accomplished in less time. Fruit is a natural source of energy for your body, whereas doughnuts have this insidious way of depleting you and your employees of the energy you need to get the job done, whether that job is brainstorming innovative ideas or conducting a productive feedback session.

I'm not promising that your feedback session will run flawlessly just because you and the other person (the one who's giving or getting feedback) ate an orange or a banana right before your meeting. But I will venture that by first getting your blood sugar to an acceptable level, both of you will be calmer, more agreeable, and better able to see each other's viewpoint. At the very least you'll both be more civil toward each other.

Make nutrition work for you. Get yourself physiologically ready before your feedback session. In my previous book, *Catchfire*, I explored in depth the relationship between nutrition and energy, energy and performance. Here are some of Tufts University's findings about the most important nutritional steps you can take:

- Start your day with a healthy breakfast.
- Set out a small tray of fruit and encourage your direct report to help himself or herself at the start of your feedback session. Have some fruit yourself. Explain the reason behind the fruit — that it'll give both of you energy while keeping you calm for a more productive session.
- If you want to serve something other than fruit, try one of these healthy options: small low-fat muffins, bagels (unless you're using the bagel as a cream cheese holder!), or yogurt.
- Keep water handy. Bottled water is practical — chances are it won't spill all over your papers like a glass of water too easily

could. Keep yourselves well hydrated before and during your feedback session. If either of you isn't getting enough water, you might end up with a headache, fatigue, or moodiness, which can lead to a lousy feedback session.

• Consider having a feedback meeting over lunch. Pick a place that offers healthy fare. Not a greasy diner. Try a restaurant with a salad bar or a light, fresh menu.

By first getting both your own and your direct report's blood sugar levels under control, you'll be able to elicit better mental and emotional responses to keep each feedback session moving in the right direction. It'll help you avoid a tense battleground. Instead you'll be creating a courteous, receptive atmosphere that makes feedback more fun, more productive, and a much more pleasant experience for everyone involved.

---

The idea for creating an energizing environment comes from Gestalt psychology, which explains how the differences in background or environment influence perception.

In her book *Mindfulness*, Harvard psychologist Ellen Langer calls this phenomenon the Power of Context.

"The way we behave in any situation has a lot to do with the context," she says. "We whisper in hospitals and become anxious in police stations, sad in cemeteries, docile in schools, and jovial at parties. Contexts control our behavior. And our mindsets determine how we interpret each context."

---

## THE RIGHT ENVIRONMENT

Ever walk into a business — could be a bank, a medical clinic, gift shop, food court, whatever — and you immediately just want to get out of there? Everything feels wrong. The lighting's awful. The music is terrible. The place looks sterile, or gloomy, or devoid of any personality. Maybe you can't quite put your finger on what's bothering you, but the atmosphere is anything but inviting.

Then there are places where you feel right at home as soon as you walk in. The energy feels good. You're relaxed and comfortable. Everything appeals to your senses. Being there just feels right.

The right environment makes a huge difference. Just ask the marketing powers-that-be at McDonald's, Starbucks, and any number of other retail establishments that are constantly looking for ways to make their environments more inviting for their customers, providing a better experience and one more likely to be repeated. Starbucks, for instance, recently introduced a major refit, adjusting the height of its counters, reorienting the relationship of its baristas to its customers, and so on.

These physical and environmental details should be kept in mind as you begin to implement your own feedback revolution. The setting where you deliver and receive feedback can go a long way toward making sure the right message gets through.

If you have a permanent office, take some steps to make it a welcoming Feedback Center — your very own Feedback Central, in fact.

Look around your office as it is now. Try to see it as others would. How does it feel to be there? Is the workplace inviting? Do people feel comfortable in your office?

Take the exercise further and ask how feedback would be received in the conference room. In their workspaces?

If none of these locations are appealing and relaxing, making them so will help set the stage beautifully for getting honest, regular feedback going.

Put some effort into improving the environment. Lighting, furniture, and décor all play a part. If interior design isn't one of your strengths, consider enlisting the help of a friend or co-worker who does have a flair for creating welcoming spaces.

# INTERLUDE

## JACK WELCH AND PETER DRUCKER:
## THE PRAGMATIST AND THE PHILOSOPHER —
## VARIATIONS ON THEMES AND VERY DIFFERENT STYLES

Jack Welch considers the lack of feedback with candor "the biggest dirty little secret in business. It blocks smart ideas, fast action, and good people contributing all the stuff they've got. It's a killer." Jack believes that most companies have some sort of system for the feedback process and the more formal reviews...which he believes should happen at least twice per year.

*Jack Welch*

His book *Winning* gives four characteristics that he believes should be part of whatever system any company has.

- It should be clear and simple. "If it involves any more than two pages of paperwork per person, something is wrong."

- It should measure people on relevant, agreed-upon criteria that relate directly to an individual's performance. He believes it should be both quantitative and qualitative on goals and behaviors. (This is very much like Peter Drucker's "Manager's Letter" written and signed by the direct report and agreed to by his/her manager.)

- As mentioned before, it should ensure that managers evaluate their people at least once a year, preferably twice, in formal, face-to-face sessions. As we describe all through *FEEDBACK REVOLUTION*, Welch believes that "informal appraisals should happen all the time."

- A good evaluation system should include a professional development component. The idea is that feedback feeds forward, and "managers should not only talk to their employees about next career steps," but also about ideas of who could replace them should they move up or out.

Peter Drucker, whom I worked with and listened to for a year at the Tarrytown 100 group meetings at Bob Swartz's Tarrytown Conference Center in New York, said something to us while drinking a German lager around the pool tables:

"A manager first and foremost must control his or her own energy, and secondly is responsible for orchestrating the energies of the people around him." He went on to say that the energy should be fueled by positive emotions rather than negative ones, though this is not always possible.

That is very philosophical and different from Jack Welch's "Four E's" of great managers...the first of which was to have Energy and secondly to Energize. (The last two Es, for those who are wondering, are to have an Edge and to Execute.) Drucker's ideas came from research and Welch's from experience, but they shared many similarities; the main one was that business was about people.

*Peter Drucker*

Drucker's ideas about feedback appraisals were expressed in *The Effective Executive*, where he said, "The appraisal tends to focus on weaknesses, not strengths — what psychologists call the 'presenting problem'. But good leaders — like good coaches — design performance processes and tasks around a person's strengths and ignore — or make irrelevant — their weaknesses."

But what he said in *The Daily Drucker* about personal feedback was that feedback is the key to continuous learning. "To know one's strengths and how to improve them, and to know what one cannot do — are the keys to continuous learning."

When building a Feedback Culture, as Jack Welch successfully did at GE while making it the biggest company in the world, one can do no better than to take the writings of both Welch and Drucker and add them to the lessons I've offered in *FEEDBACK REVOLUTION*, building them into your core values. It will take time, but it will be worth it.

Just as monitoring your blood sugar helps you maintain "interior" energy levels, *feng shui* provides you with an exterior environment that serves your wellbeing. *Feng shui*, which I like to call "acupuncture for architecture," is all about creating a safe, comfortable physical place, or "exterior" calm energy. Simple changes in lighting, furnishings, décor, and furniture placement can make a huge difference, turning a once uncomfortable area into a place where everybody wants to be. Create an environment conducive to feedback.

## FEEDBACK LOG: PETER

A number of years ago, I was working as a consultant to Dale Tooley, one of Denver's legendary District Attorneys. After his election, he decided to add some flavor to his office. A DA has plenty of power and, as Ellen Langer pointed out in the quote above, people freeze up when they come into the DA's office...including some of the assistant DAs and the District Attorney's staff as well. He needed a place conducive to the public and for meeting with his staff in small groups or one-on-one discussion and feedback sessions.

The idea we came up with was to defuse some of that "I'm the DA and you're not!" feeling.

So he moved the big desk to the corner and used it only as his writing desk. In the middle of the room he placed a round table and chairs. (Round tables are inclusive and encourage dialogue.) He brightened the lighting and most days had flowers in the room.

On the round table, he had a bowl of jelly beans that he offered to those in attendance. (I, of course, pushed for fruit instead of candy, but the DA's budget didn't allow for that.) The results were predictable: Energy levels were high, creativity abounded, and he was able

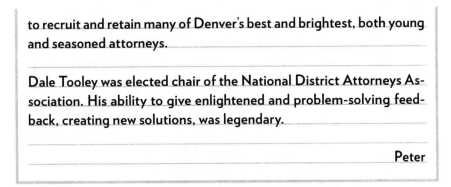

to recruit and retain many of Denver's best and brightest, both young and seasoned attorneys.

Dale Tooley was elected chair of the National District Attorneys Association. His ability to give enlightened and problem-solving feedback, creating new solutions, was legendary.

Peter

William R. Hewlett, cofounder of the Hewlett-Packard Company (now known as HP), once said,

*"Men and women want to do a good job, and if they are provided the proper environment, they will do so."*

Same with feedback. Create the right environment to deliver and receive feedback, and you'll not only get more open and honest feedback from everyone you work with, but you'll also feel better, happier, and more focused yourself. An environment that's ideal for a 45- minute feedback session will deliver other benefits to you all day long.

*Feng shui* ("wind and water") is an ancient Chinese practice of orienting buildings in ways that increase the amount of positive energy. The concept has been adopted — and adapted — by architects and interior designers to accommodate placement of furniture, open spaces, artwork, and virtually every element of workplace or home.

Too "New Agey" for business? I had the same concerns when I recommended that my client Visteon, the multinational auto parts manufacturer, consider hiring a *feng shui* master to review their plans for an expansion of one of their facilities.

Perhaps surprising both of us, the executive VP in charge of the project did just that, and the *feng shui* master made suggestions and provided ideas that were incorporated into the new facility to great effect.

Now take a look at your own workspace — or whatever location you most frequently use for providing and receiving feedback. You don't have to hire a *feng shui* master — just look at Dale Tooley's simple plan from above: Make changes that increase the welcoming nature — and energy levels — of your office, conference room, or other space.

# WALK YOUR TALK — THE OUTDOORS AS FEEDBACK ENVIRONMENT

If you don't have an office, or a convenient location that you can sculpt into your own Feedback Central, scout out locations suitable for your feedback conversation.

Some of the best-received feedback I've ever presented has been delivered during walks through public parks and other open spaces. Perhaps your company already has such a space. Siemens, Apple, and Navistar, three corporations I've worked with on feedback issues, have attractive corporate campuses replete with pleasant walking paths that are ideal for feedback sessions.

For those who don't have a well-designed corporate campus handy, other good locations include:

- Public libraries — most of which have comfortable corners where you are allowed to talk (although softly).
- Private dining areas at restaurants. (Remember the Swedish executive who always took employees to a fine restaurant, especially when he had to deliver disturbing news.)
- Scenic overlooks and picnic areas, if convenient to the workplace.
- Community college and university meeting rooms that are available to the public.

The point is that a little effort will enable you to find the perfect setting for your feedback/dialogue.

Once you've got the spot set up, just what are you going to do in Feedback Central?

## FEEDBACK LOG: PETER

"Surprise feedback" has its place, as I learned from Coach Shanahan while I observed a Denver Broncos practice session during the dog days of August. Now imagine how a day like that affects a football team being put through an intense practice session.

Hot, sweaty, and tired from working their butts off, the players were digging deep for the energy to run the next play when an air horn blasted through the heat, calling their attention to a couple of carts that had been wheeled onto the field.

The carts were laden with popsicles, and the thought of the frozen treats inspired a team of weary, sweat-drenched football millionaires to find the energy to race one another to claim their favorite flavors and colors.

Once in a while, more often than you think, feedback can be fun.

And once in a while, when the time is right, feedback should be fun!

Peter

# FORMAL FEEDBACK SESSIONS — THE PERFORMANCE REVIEW

I've focused here on setting up lengthier and more formal feedback sessions, whether they're in your office or someplace where you and the other party will get a measure of privacy, because these are, after all, the feedback sessions most of us remember most clearly:

- Performance reviews
- Promotions
- Corrective or negative feedback sessions
- Disciplinary sessions

Corrective and disciplinary sessions are out of the ordinary, and tend not to be scheduled far in advance. Promotions are more rare than most of us wish. So we're talking here about formal performance reviews, which for most of us is an annual occurrence.

They are a great opportunity for in-depth feedback. During the performance review you can dig deeper, discover and discuss perhaps overlooked or unknown areas of concern (and optimism!), and explore them in detail. The annual performance review is a highly important event and deserves the time, preparation, reflection, and concentration required to honor its importance as well as that of its recipient.

It's a shame, in many ways, that this event occurs only once a year. But for many of us, that *annual* review is a matter of company policy, a carefully scheduled element of a Performance Management System.

## HOW MANY FORMAL REVIEWS DO YOU NEED EACH YEAR?

I believe you need to do four formal, well-prepared feedback sessions a year with each of your direct reports. One session per quarter. And you need to put it on the calendar at the start of the year so that everyone knows it's going to happen and everyone knows when it's coming up.

I can't stress this enough. If company policy permits, I urge you to schedule quarterly reviews. Why four times a year? I believe it's hard to give good feedback — and by doing so, subtly persuade your team members that they, too, can love feedback — unless you do it every three months, or thereabouts, because otherwise you simply forget too much. Your team members want to know:
- Am I doing things right?
- Am I on the right track?
- What's going on?

And you want to keep your direct report in the loop. All of which point to the fact that annual feedback sessions are insufficient. Quarterly reviews are essential.

In my opinion.

Name _____ Date _____

**iLoveFeedback**©
*worksheet*

Feedback Opportunity _____

**1. Find your Zone.**

Energy: _____ Attitude: _____ Environment: _____

_____ _____ _____

**2. Get Smart.**

What is the intent? _____

What's in it for them? (WIIFT) _____

**3. Create the Message.**

What did you observe? _____

What words would you use to clearly articulate how this behavior gets in the way of, or promotes, this person's success?

_____

**4. Deliver the Feedback.**

How will you ask for permission? _____

What is your statement of appreciation? _____

Share the feedback, as recorded above in Step 3: Create the Message.

**5. Encourage, Energize, & End Well.**

How would you offer support? _____

What is an open-ended question you might need to ask? _____

What non-verbals will you watch in yourself and the other person? _____

What are action items and deadlines? _____

What could you say when you thank the other person? _____

www.ilovefeedback.com • 303-796-0444

Whatever the frequency of the formal performance review, you need to
- Put on your Formal Feedback oxygen mask first.
- Find your Feedback Zone.

Then prepare for the session:
- Your **iLoveFeedback** Worksheet is an invaluable tool. Review your annotations for the person in question.
- If you don't have an **iLoveFeedback** Worksheet, carefully review your notes on the other person's past reviews beforehand.

- Look back through your feedback logs, journal, or notebook — any good information there that you'll want to bring into the session?
- Review what you both discussed during the previous session.
- Review your notes from the previous session.

Do your homework, and you'll find that things will go more smoothly. Far more importantly, you are honoring the responsibility that a formal performance review requires.

## FEEDBACK ON THE FLY

There's more than formality and scheduled performance reviews to good feedback — lots more.

And one of the best and most effective types of feedback is what I call *Feedback on the Fly* — both the casual type of feedback where you just drop by and share a few thoughts, and the more critical but equally unscheduled feedback that arises from crunch times, project deadlines, preparation for vacations and holidays, and other intense times at your company.

This type of feedback is informal, your delivery is casual (except, probably, during those crunch times), and your tone typically is light.

A casual Feedback on the Fly session might happen something like this: You drop by your direct report's office and, as a way of asking permission, inquire if you could have a minute of his or her time. If they say, "Now's not a good time," then simply ask when would be a better time. But if they say, "Sure, come on in," you've got the green light to deliver casual feedback.

Here are examples of what you might say:

- Great job running the status meeting today! I like how you kept things moving along and how you asked for everyone's input. I'd like to make just one suggestion. We've got a couple of less expressive people on the team who aren't going to speak up necessarily, but they've got great ideas to share. So at the next meeting, how about trying this: After everyone's had a chance to talk, address the folks who haven't spoken and ask them directly, "Is there anything you'd like to add?" That might get them to open up. What do you think?

- You did a brilliant job negotiating that deal this afternoon! I just want to say thank you. Good work!

- I'm putting together a "phone courtesy" checklist for our team to follow, and I'd like your feedback. Could you take a minute to look this over? What am I missing?

- Your work is excellent, but you tend to slip into meetings late. I understand that your individual thinking style doesn't naturally pay attention to schedules, but I also want you to bear in mind that whatever else you are thinking about, promptness at meetings is an important aspect of teamwork, and teamwork is as important to our business as individual initiative, creativity, and other aspects of the important contributions you make to the company. In other words, I want you to put your whole brain to work.

In each of these cases, there's no need to schedule a formal sit-down session. Just a few minutes of your direct report's time and a casual approach are all that's required. You can give and receive informal feedback in this manner regularly. Opportunities will appear at least weekly, for many of you daily, and for some of you several times each day.

It's good to give praise both formally and informally. The nice thing about praising someone informally is that usually others are within earshot, which guarantees that coworkers will overhear you. This strategy works well all the way around. First, your direct report feels good about having colleagues hear about his or her accomplishments. And second, everyone else will be motivated to do a good job in order to get public praise from you.

Frankly, this strategy, which most of us have seen in practice, can be dramatically improved by actually calling attention to itself.

Say you want to give someone on your team a bit of unscheduled but well-deserved praise. Call attention to it! Try something like this:

*"Everybody gather round! This won't take long, but I wanted all of you to know what a sterling job Shirley has been doing lately, and specifically on the three-month printing schedule. The feedback she gave on the new process was exactly what we needed to improve efficiency by 4%!*

*"Let's have a round of applause for Shirley!"*

On the other hand, try not to give negative feedback in front of others. This you always have to do in private. You gain nothing by embarrassing your direct report in front of his peers. You don't want to create that kind of divisive, negative atmosphere at work.

But as we saw in Chapter Three, a measurably higher number of positives to every negative will temper critical feedback and make it far more effective — a benefit that can be wholly defeated by delivering the feedback with an audience beyond its intended one.

Informal feedback can take on other forms too — a casual conversation in the hallways or at lunch, an email, a message scribbled on a sticky note. Informal feedback is something you can give often, anywhere, and everywhere, using a variety of methods. It's especially good for discussing project details, reviewing milestones, and throwing around general ideas.

## TIPS, TOOLS, & TACTICS

**TIP:** Look at your workplace with the eyes of the recipient of your feedback. How would the setting make you *feel* if you were invited into it for a dialogue with a supervisor or manager, or a direct report?

**TIP:** Spend one day tracking your eating habits and reflecting on how those habits affect your energy, focus, and productivity. An understanding of your blood sugar levels might well be as important as understanding the work you are doing.

**TIP:** Try not to give negative feedback in front of others. (If you are feeling anxious, you will probably give negative feedback without thinking.)

**TIP:** Be alert for "Feedback on the Fly" opportunities — and don't let them pass! Remember: Unlike good red wine, feedback doesn't "keep."

TOOL: Use your iLoveFeedback notepad to prepare for performance reviews, of course — but also look at specific entries from time to time *between* performance reviews, adding notes and making adjustments as necessary, based on performance observations since the most recent review.

TOOL: Take a moment to inspect the lighting, seating, and other appointments if your workspace. Could anything be changed to make the space more appealing and inviting, better able to provide the relaxed and at the same time energized atmosphere that makes for great and effective feedback?

TOOL: Follow up Feedback on the Fly with a brief written note, card, or email, reminding the recipient of the feedback you delivered.

TACTIC: Be attentive to time of day and energy levels when offering feedback. This applies to feedback offered to direct reports or superiors.

TACTIC: Develop a good sense of the daily rhythms and how energy levels rise and fall among the people you provide feedback to. Time your feedback sessions accordingly.

TACTIC: Keep in mind the need for a higher percentage of positive to negative feedback, for Feedback on the Fly, just as you would for more formal feedback sessions.

# CODA

Coda, Italian for "tail," is also a musical term that designates a musical passage that brings the whole piece to an end.

The coda offers a "look back and take it all in" moment...savor it and its meaning. The equivalent in film would be going from an emotional close-up to a contextual long shot of the entire scene, a kind of summing up.

That's what this coda is all about.

*One evening an old Cherokee told his grandson about a battle that is waged within all people. "There is a war between two wolves who dwell within each of us," he said, and went on to explain:*

*"One wolf is Negativity. It is anger, sadness, stress, fear, guilt, and shame.*

*"The other wolf is Positivity. It is joy, gratitude, interest, optimism, and above all, love."*

*The grandson thought about it for a minute and then asked his grandfather:*

*"Which wolf wins?"*

*The old Cherokee replied simply, "The one you feed."*

You can't change the past, but you can learn from it.

And the lessons you learn can help shape the future.

As I've shown through this book, effective feedback is *always* aimed at the future.

This is true of even the most "past-performance" focused feedback sessions. Whether seeking to address or correct a problem, increase productivity or improve sales, adjust for changing conditions or introduce a shift in strategy, you will find that effective, well-played feedback:

- Identifies the specific problem or situation, and ensures that the recipient understands it
- Examines the specific "whys and hows" of the subject
- Defines the parameters and particulars of the changes needed to correct the problem or address the situation
- Moves quickly and positively to the future benefits of the changes at hand

The emphasis is on the positive nature of the future that will be produced as a result of the feedback and the actions the recipient takes based on that feedback.

In the course of accomplishing these goals, effective feedback also communicates and displays cardinal virtues:

- Feedback is candid in environments where real candor is crucial yet not often practiced.
- Feedback is civil in an age when civility is sadly on the wane.
- Feedback is gracious and inviting, even when addressing serious problems or situations.

This approach and the commitment that underlies it are so compellingly straightforward, with such broad and demonstrable results, that I remain startled that so many companies, organizations, and institutions continue to neglect, misunderstand, and above all, ignore the practice of effective feedback within their ranks.

It is my hope and belief that *Feedback Revolution* is large step toward remedying that situation. I hope, in fact, that feedback becomes as common and important a watchword in business as "excellence," which was, frankly, a word not often heard in business circles before Tom Peters, in his bestselling book, *In Search of Excellence*, pointed out that excellence was what all successful companies were pursuing. Peters introduced people to a new way of thinking about a familiar word, and in doing so turned that familiar word into what was for many a new concept.

My goal with *Feedback Revolution* has been to awaken you to a new way of thinking about a familiar word: **feedback**. In the case of feedback, that familiarity has bred misunderstanding, apprehension and anxiety, and an often total avoidance of the subject.

Now that you've read the book, I trust that your sense of what effective feedback is  and isn't — has been transformed. During my years of work on this subject, as a speaker, consultant, and writer, I found that the transformation of a familiar word into a far-reaching concept offered constant insights. I saw — as I believe you will too — feedback all around me. We live in a feedback-driven environment, from GPS systems to stoplights to reality TV and sporting events to political campaigns to "Like" buttons and online comments to all the other examples and incidents of feedback — whether effective or not — that we encounter as we move through our days and nights.

The best of it, the most effective and worthwhile feedback, always faces forward, always addresses the future. A feedback-driven performance review, for instance, is also a performance preview: This is where you have been, this is what you have accomplished, this is where you are going, and this what you are *going to accomplish and how you are going to accomplish it.*

That's effective feedback.

---

The goal of this book is to bring a real and wide awareness of feedback as "the elephant in the room" of most corporate cultures.

Awareness is the vital first step in all change.

By applying our awareness of the need for a Feedback Revolution to changing our attitudes toward feedback from negative to positive, we take the equally vital next step toward making our Feedback Revolution a reality.

---

Several times during this book I've talked about "feed-forward" as one of the key attributes of effective, worthwhile, productive feedback.

Over the decades that I've used the term "feed-forward" in my speeches and consulting engagements, it has always earned smiles and nods of comprehension and dawning understanding. Other writers — Marshall Goldsmith, author of many books, *What Got You Here Won't Get You There* notable among them — have made similar points: Effective feedback always feeds forward.

It should be clear that this book is itself an in-depth feedback session directed at the idea of feedback, particularly feedback as it is often (mal)practiced in business and organizations. But my intent, as with any well-practiced bit of feedback, is not to dwell on the malpractice, not to focus on the mistakes or avoidances, other than to make clear that we can do better, and to show the elements and approaches that enable us to do so.

The result, I hope, is a positive, practical, comprehensive, and, yes, revolutionary approach to feedback that will have the effect of transforming the way you think about feedback and, as consequence, transforming the way you practice feedback in your company.

And because I believe deeply in practicing what I preach, I'd like you to let me know how I did. Give me your feedback on this book and the concepts, approaches, strategies, tools, practices, and ideas I've presented here.

How are *you* using the book?

What shape is *your* feedback revolution taking?

How has your team, and your organization, responded to that feedback revolution?

What's the current status of your company's Feedback Culture? Where do you see that culture headed in the future?

Let me know — give me your feedback.

And allow me to give you my very best wishes for the continued success, evolution, and growth of your feedback revolution and the business and the people it serves and its benefits today — and tomorrow and tomorrow.

*Peter McLaughlin*

# AFTERWORD

# THE ORIGINS AND GROWTH OF THE *ILOVEFEEDBACK* TRAINING PROGRAM

**By Marjorie Mauldin, Founder and President Executive Forum, and Co-creator, with Peter McLaughlin, of the *iLove Feedback* Program**

I founded Executive Forum in order to offer Colorado's leading executives and managers including representatives of Martin Marietta, Gates Rubber Co., Ball Aerospace and others, the opportunity to come together and hear speakers on relevant subjects, as well as follow-up programs exploring those subjects in greater depth and detail. All of us at Executive Forum were excited when we booked Peter McLaughlin to deliver his "Power of Feedback" presentation.. We were aware of the amount of research into feedback that Peter had been doing, and suspected that his presentation would attract a lot of attention.

Because of the number of pre-registrations, we knew even before the presentation that the "Power of Feedback" was going to be popular. It proved to be more than that. Peter's presentation lasted three hours, yet the audience of executives and managers wanted more. They could see the value of effective feedback as a vital element in their leadership toolbox, and they let us know that they wanted, more than ever, to learn the skills involved in creating effective feedback.

It was clear to me that there was a need for a formal feedback training program, and after a comprehensive search, we could not find a training program that delivered the feedback message we thought was so vitally important. I suggested to Peter that we try on the idea of developing a feedback program that emphasized positive psychology, as well as offering practical, how-to, and step-by-step instruction. Conversations and ideas began to flow.

As we developed our parameters, we also began to consider the purposes we wanted the program to achieve. We knew we wanted participants to have a paradigm shift in the way they viewed feedback — what Peter so aptly labels a *Feedback Revolution*. We wanted them to become known in their companies as leaders who actually looked forward to the performance appraisal process. We wanted them to love giving feedback! However, we only really love activities in which we are very competent. Competence comes from study and applied practice – and that is what we wanted to deliver to business people all over the world.

At the same time, we wanted the training program to be practical, fun, include a logical model, and allow participants to apply their knowledge to a real time situation. Drawing on my background in instructional design and adult learning theory, we worked hard to include basic learning principles.

We knew the program must be goal oriented. Participants would need to learn new information and skills and have an opportunity to practice the skills, so that they would be confident of their ability to put them to work. We also wanted to "practice what we preach" by using positive psychology.

The Five Best Practice Steps were developed over time, using a panel of subject matter experts. This design team met once a month for over a year to debate and develop the elements of the model. We really went about this in a practical way – if we were going to deliver the most effective feedback session – how would that take place? What steps would you take? Would there be a model, how many steps, should it be 3, 5, 7? We experimented with various options and configurations, and the program began to take shape.Special thanks goes to Beth Wolfson and Alana Berlund who helped lead the process.

We used several different client groups to pilot both the instructional design and the use of the workbook. The participants were very helpful and gave us great suggestions to refine the content and the workbook. In fact, it was in the pilot session where we narrowed the best practice steps to five when we combined encourage, energize and end well into step five. We also took the advice of a participant to try to limit the writing in the book to the lower half – making it easier to write in.

We had a huge success when Comcast decided to train 800 call center managers in the **iLove Feedback** program. Their training manager was very intent on changing the culture within the call centers and developing a program to decrease turn-over.

By now we have trained thousands of people, with the number growing constantly.

But more importantly, the organizations who are using **iLoveFeedback** in their training program are driving change in a number of areas.

To give just one example, a government agency is using **iLoveFeedback** training to help managers and directors communicate an important policy change to employees. The agency was experiencing inflated ratings – meaning, over 75% of employees were receiving the highest rating. Agency executives made a decision to require a new level of documentation for any performance appraisals that gave employees the highest rating. Employees didn't understand why they wouldn't be given the same rating they had received in the previous cycle.

**iLoveFeedback** training was used to develop the skills to give honest and accurate feedback to employees.

And that's just one of hundreds of specific uses of **iLoveFeedback** training in an organization.

As Peter shows in *Feedback Revolution*, examples of effective feedback are all around us – and we all need to get better at this vital and basic communication skill. The business world is moving at a much faster pace than ever before. Our technology and tools enable quick decision making and collaboration.

The ability of managers, leaders and teams to keep up with this pace is dependent on learning and using higher level communication skills such as giving effective feedback to encourage and build employee capacity.

We have a lofty goal – one beautifully presented in *Feedback Revolution* as well as our **iLoveFeedback** program.

That goal is to equip all leaders with the ability to feel confident and competent when giving feedback. As we've seen with **iLoveFeedback** program participants, and as readers of Peter's book will discover, the benefits of this *Feedback Revolution* begin to flow throughout every aspect of the company. And their benefits will continue to flow as recipients of better and more effective feedback come to love it themselves.

Margie

# ACKNOWLEDGMENTS

"**S**ine qua non" is an old Latin phrase meaning "that without which." In the writing of this book there are some "those without whom" this book would not have come to fruition. I thank them deeply.

My son Peter McLaughlin, former head of research and development for McLaughlin Company, who worked with me to produce the original "Power of Feedback" training program for a Fortune 200 company, from which the original manuscript evolved.

Margie Mauldin, founder and CEO of Executive Forum, who took the wheel as we worked together to develop the **iLoveFeedback** training program, and added much to the book itself. (You'll see some of her stories in her Feedback Logs throughout the book.) To find out more about the **iLoveFeedback** training program, see the information pages at the back of the book. Alana Berland of Executive Forum was indispensible in implementing the **iLoveFeedback** program and overseeing its rapid growth and ongoing popularity.

And ultimate thanks to Keith Ferrell, former Editor in Chief of *Omni* Magazine, and who has the title of Editor here, but is in fact co-producer of *FEEDBACK REVOLUTION*. We wrote and researched virtually, for two years to bring this book to fruition...it is a product of Feed "back and forth and forth and back., without our ever meeting in person, a situation we intend to rectify soon. Keith is a formidable author in his own right in history, science, science fiction, and novels, including *Passing Judgment*. We had a huge amount of fun getting off track on movies, classical music, literature and science...and still managed daily focus on this book's development and evolution.

Thanks to John McLaughlin, my (Heavy Metal music reviewer and editor) son, who always reads and corrects much of what I write; and my daughter, Jennifer Calderon, who also read the manuscript and commented on both the content and marketing from her vantage point as an author of four books herself, including *That White Girl,* soon to become a movie. The *abuelo* thanks Gabriel and Camilo for constant, honest, and fun feedback.

Gratitude goes to Jeff Howard, my partner in our sales training company, Winning Sales Habits, who added his talents as COO, web orchestrator, and problem solver. He has also worked on every facet of this project from the beginning.

Dr. Steve Forness, Ph.D., Distinguished Professor Emeritus, UCLA — thanks, Steve, for being first reader of the manuscript, and adding new ways to think about the topic — and always with great fun.

Dr, Geil Browning, Ph.D, author of *Emergenetics*™ and CEO of Emergenetics™ International, gets a round of applause and thanks for reading and editing our important chapter "This is Your Brain on Feedback" which relies heavily on her book and research in neuroscience and psychology.

Dr. Martin Seligman, Ph.D., Zellerbach Family Professor of Psychology, Department of Psychology, University of Pennsylvania — our lunch at Wharton kicked off the third chapter of this book, "Real. Positive. Feedback."

A thank you to Jim Gibbons, CEO of Goodwill International, both friend and client, for helping clarify my thinking on feedback.

I raise a glass of Apple Beer with gratitude to Larry Stillman. The most positive person I know — investor and philanthropist, and great giver of feedback.

Don Cunningham, splendid golfer, wine drinker, and Beethoven lover read the book and gave me feedback on everything from content to grammar.

David A. French, founder of Orbis Institute, has supported this venture with both intellectual and financial capital, all with outrageous humor.

I am gratified by and appreciative of the Board of Directors of Explorers Foundation, including Chairman Ed Warner and President Leif Smith who most unexpectedly presented me with a Cobden-Bright Award. I will let their citation speak for them:

> Explorers Foundation Presents a Cobden-Bright Award to Peter McLaughlin, author of Feedback Revolution
>
> Explorers Foundation invests in ideas that contribute to a world fit for explorers, and that help people prepare themselves to flourish in a rapidly changing world.
>
> Cobden-Bright awards are named in honor of two successful removers of barriers to constructive human actions, Richard Cobden and John Bright, both of mid-19th century England.
>
> Peter McLaughlin's work contributes to our purposes by providing people within large organizations the ideas, stories, and opportunities for action that, taken as a whole, result in an improved fit between growing human capacity and a challenging world. Feedback Revolution offers a new approach to the exchange of positive and negative information among participants in organizations. We are pleased that our $2,500 award will hasten publication.
>
> Among previous recipients of Cobden-Bright awards have been Sand County Foundation; Alan Macfarlane, Emeritus Professor, Department of Social Anthropology, King's College, Cambridge; and co-authors of America 3.0, James C. Bennett and Michael J. Lotus.

I am grateful to the wizard of "computery," Emily Holleran, Director of Operations for McLaughlin Company for sticking with this from the beginning, putting together most all of the PowerPoints and just about *everything* else.

Thanks to Shannon McLaughlin, my daughter-in-law, for her observations coming from her managerial experience, and for preparing great food while doing so.

"Grazie mile" to Riccardo Mazzeo, MBA, and honcho at 3 Tomatoes Catering, for looking at the manuscript from a "business perspective," and for both Riccardo and Deana for being trusted and fun friends.

And to Joahna McKinley, the most friendly and efficient giver of candid feedback in the family. She can nod her head yes, while still saying no.

A note of appreciation to Pat Wagner, founder of Siera: LearnTeach. Inspire. for years of constructive feedback, always practical, always fun.

Appreciation to Dan Meyer, co-author of BEAT THE EXIT BUBBLE, for the idea sessions and events he got me involved with and his always positive feedback.

Tom and Beth Behnke, thanks for all the help you both gave me at the beginning of the Feedback process...cheers

A special thanks to Barry Elson, former Executive VP at Cox Communications, for giving me feedback I really wasn't looking for, but helped me change some important concepts

The Candor in Feedback Award goes to Dr. Ken Petri who gave me his absolutely candid and pointed comments on the manuscripts, and made it better by doing so.

Steve Brazell, CEO of Hitman Inc., a competition removal company, who designed the book cover to all of the chapter templates.

Steve's great design was transmuted into the gorgeous reality you're reading by the gifted Barbara Alber. My thanks to her for her superb work.

Super copy editor Dave Baker saw to it that the book is consistent and correct in matters of grammar.

E-book readers can thank Dustin Carpenter for the fine job he did formatting the book for various devices.

My thanks to J. G. Sauls, Dan Smith, and Josh Viola for reading the manuscript and giving me their insights and impressions. Steffie Allen, Madie Gustafson, and Sharyl Harston provided insightful and entertaining conversations about Feedback Revolution for which I am grateful.

# PHOTO CREDITS

*Peter McLaughlin partners with two organizations mentioned in this book, offering targeted programs:*

Feedback is "the Breakfast of Champions." It creates a culture of Kaizen, making frequent small adjustments, stepping back and seeing what changed, making other small adjustments, and continuing the process. By offering feedback individuals and organizations can optimize performance and accelerate results.

Then why are 'feedback' or 'performance review' such negative terms?

**iLoveFeedback** is a course, and a way of thinking about feedback to improve results and relationships at work and with the people around you. Clients include Comcast, Dish/EchoStar, Sharp Healthcare, Visteon and HUD.

For more information on iLoveFeedback, co-created by Peter McLaughlin and Marjorie Mauldin, visit the following Web address:
   **http://ilovefeedback.com/**

## EXECUTIVE FORUM

For more information on other programs offered by Executive Forum, visit:
   **www.executiveforum.net/**

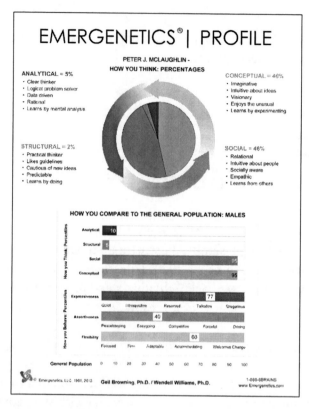

Technically, *Emergenetics* is a brain-based psychometric assessment that highlights thinking and behavior. In practice . . . it's clarity. Simply, *Emergenetics* is a clearer understanding of how people live, work, communicate and interact.

Peter has successfully used the Emergenetics Profile to help many companies, including IBM, Goodwill International, Sharp Health, Great West Life, Coors, and Smith-Barney.

For more information, visit the following Web address:

### www.petermclaughlin.com/emergenetics.html

# PETER MCLAUGHLIN
# AND THE
# MCLAUGHLIN COMPANY

With its popular and effective

- ☑ SPEECHES
- ☑ SEMINARS
- ☑ KEYNOTES
- ☑ EXECUTIVE COACHING
- ☑ and
- ☑ CUSTOM PROGRAMS ...

The McLaughlin Company has helped a wide variety of business and institutional clients develop, deploy, and sustain the sets of tools that enable their employees to perform better.

Those tools include seminars and speeches addressing:

**THE FEEDBACK REVOLUTION —**
*10 Tools for Creating and Delivering Feedback that Works!*

**CATCHFIRE! —**
*How to Ignite Energy, Defuse Stress, and Power Boost Performance !*

**BRAINSTYLES —**
*Understanding the Way People Think and Behave Can Transform Your Business and Professional Relationships*

Find out more at The McLaughlin Company's Web site:

**http://www.petermclaughlin.com/**

## PETER McLAUGHLIN KEEPS VERY GOOD COMPANY:

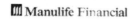

## AND THESE ARE JUST SOME OF THE NICE THINGS THEY SAY ABOUT HIM:

"*Peter McLaughlin was simply fantastic. His program has spurred dramatic improvements in the personal and professional lives of everyone who attended.*"

Marie Amoruso, Director of Planning, Apple Computer

"*Thanks for the fine job you did as keynote speaker for our Symposium. Your message was right on target and entertaining. We have received many favorable comments...I would like to continue to work with you to ensure that we follow up with a systematic program...Thanks again for helping us make this the most successful Symposium ever.*"

William Slavin, Vice President, IBM Global Services

"*I have now received all of the feedback from your speech...and Peter McLaughlin got RAVE REVIEWS! ...Thanks again and I look forward to getting you back in front of my team.*"

James F. Flaherty,
Managing Director of Investment Banking, Merrill Lynch

"THANKS! I read your book, CatchFire, a few months ago and was so taken by it I arranged the class you taught to my Intel team a few weeks back. Just wanted to drop a note of thanks to you and your team, everyone here is still raving about the class and the continued impact it has had on their lives."

Channel Marketing Manager, Intel

"The program was a huge success. Feedback on the evaluations tells me that it was one of the consistently highest rated programs we've had. We will call you about coming back."

Andrew Shiel, Education Chairman.
Young Presidents Organization (YPO)

"On behalf of all of us at American Express Real Estate Services, I would like to thank you for a wonderful presentation at our conference last week...I believe that our group will utilize this experience to significantly improve how they approach and work with our customers...Thank you again for contributing to what was an extremely successful annual meeting."

John K. Powell, Vice President, American Express

**And about the program that led to this book:**

"Feedback Revolution is a winner, as viewed by my management team of Vice Presidents, Directors, Managers and Supervisors at Sharp Community Medical Group.

The process for giving feedback is a simple and reproducible tool for all aspects of communication where one is challenged on how to deliver a message or give feedback that will be well received, but more importantly improve   individual and therefore the organizations overall success."

John E. Jenrette MD. Chief Executive,
Sharp Community Medical Group

"Thank you for your entertaining presentation on The Power of Feedback. I was fortunate enough to be able to attend, and found myself recommending your tips and recommendations to friends and colleagues. I believe the feedback message invaluable, and trust that those of us who attended the session are practicing the lessons learned to foster a company that embraces the 'Power of Feedback.'"

Elaine T. Cloutier, Lean Six Sigma Coordinator, Visteon


*Peter would love to hear from YOU:*

email: Peter@petermclaughlin.com

(303) 321-5008

www.petermclaughlin.com/contact.html

THE McLAUGHLIN COMPANY

CPSIA information can be obtained at www.ICGtesting.com
Printed in the USA
LVOW09s1619311014

411461LV00015B/634/P